Print-On-Demand Mastery

The Ultimate Blueprint for Print-On-Demand Success—An Actionable Step-By-Step Strategy for Building, Launching, Marketing, and Maintaining a Profitable Print-On-Demand Business

By Change Your Life Guru

Books by **Change Your Life Guru**:

Affiliate Marketing Mastery: *The Ultimate Guide to Starting Your Online Business and Earning Passive Income - Unlock Profitable Affiliate Secrets, Boost Earnings with Expert Strategies, Top Niches, High-Performance Products, Innovative Tactics and Essential Tools for Success*

Dropshipping Business Mastery: *The Ultimate Guide to Starting & Managing a Thriving Dropshipping Business - Skyrocket Your Income with Proven Strategies, Profitable Niches, and Unleash Powerful Marketing Tactics*

Etsy Store Mastery: *The Ultimate Guide to Building Your Own Etsy Empire - Learn Proven Strategies for Finding & Selling the Hottest Products, Building Your Brand, and Dominating Your Niche on Etsy*

Online Course Mastery: *The Ultimate Guide to Creating and Marketing Profitable Online Courses - Learn How to Find Your Niche, Create Engaging Content, and Succeed as an Online Course Creator*

Online Freelancing Mastery: *The Ultimate Guide to Making Money as an Online Freelancer - Unlock Proven Strategies to Monetize Your Skills and Talents, Market Yourself, and Go from Zero To Success*

Online Tutoring: *The Ultimate Guide to Creating a Profitable Online Tutoring Business – Become an Expert in Your Niche, Craft Engaging Sessions, Harness Powerful Marketing Strategies, and Profit from Your Expertise in the Digital Learning World*

Print on Demand Mastery: *The Ultimate Blueprint for Print on Demand Success - Unlock Actionable Tips & Strategies to Starting, Setting Up, and Marketing a Profitable Print on Demand Business*

Social Media Influencer: *The Ultimate Guide to Building a Profitable Social Media Influencer Career - Learn How to Build Your Brand, Create Viral Content, and Make Brands Beg to Pay for Your Lifestyle*

Subscription Business Model: *The Ultimate Guide to Building and Scaling A Predictable Recurring Income Business - Attract and Retain Loyal Subscribers, and Maximize Your Profitability with Proven Strategies and Best Practices*

YouTube Influencer: *The Ultimate Guide to YouTube Success, Content Creation, and Monetization Strategies - Build and Grow a Thriving YouTube Channel and Boost Engagement with Proven Techniques and Insider Secrets*

THANK YOU – A Gift For You!

THANK YOU for purchasing our book! *You could have chosen from dozens of other books on the same topic but you took a chance and chose this one.* As a token of our appreciation, we would like to offer you an exclusive **FREE GIFT BOX**. Your Gift Box contains powerful downloadable products, resources and tools that are the perfect companion to your newly-acquired book, and are designed to catapult you towards freedom and success.

To get instant access, just go to:
https://changeyourlife.guru/toolkit

Inside your Free Gift Box, you'll receive:

- **Goal Planners and Schedulers**: Map out manageable and actionable steps so you have clarity and are empowered with a clear roadmap to achieve every goal.

- **Expert Tips & Tricks:** Invaluable tips and strategies ready to apply to your life, or business, to accelerate your progress and reach your outcomes.

- **Exclusive Content:** Free bonus materials, resources, and tools to help you succeed.

- **New Freebies:** Enter your email address to download your free gift box and be updated when we add new Free Content, ensuring you always have the tools, information and strategies to sky-rocket your success!

Are you ready to supercharge your life? Download your gift box for FREE today! [**https://changeyourlife.guru/toolkit**]

Table of Contents

Introduction

Guy Kawasaki once said, "Ideas are easy. Implementation is hard". It's easy to decide to start a print-on-demand (PoD) business—a business in which you create the product once the customer has bought it. What can be challenging is implementing your PoD idea. The major issue is having the right mindset and knowledge to make your idea work. That's why you should start by gathering the knowledge and then implementing what you learn.

Why should you start a PoD business? For starters, a PoD business is a great side hustle to launch because of its low upfront costs. When you start a business, it's preferable to go into a large and growing industry. Most importantly, you want to start a business that's connected with your passions and interests. This helps you stay excited even when you encounter inevitable challenging times. Does a PoD business meet the requirements we've just stated?

The market value of the PoD industry in 2022 stood at $5.4 billion globally. It's estimated that it'll hit $39 billion by 2031, which means it'll have a compound annual growth of about 26.2%. This is exciting news for anyone interested in entering this industry. The PoD value is so large, you don't need to have a huge market share to make thousands of dollars. For example, if the market value of this industry is $7 billion, and you gain a 0.00001% market share annually, you'll make $70,000 per year.

Can this growth be sustained over the long term? The answer is yes, and here's why. Many consumers prefer to appear unique and want products that confirm this desire. This desire has existed for as long as humans have been on this planet. Who doesn't want to feel unique and important? The PoD industry specializes in offering personalized products and taps into this desire. You can expect the demand for customized products to remain for a long time. The demand for personalized products provides the opportunity to make money now and in the future.

The modern PoD business runs online. As more and more people are accessing the internet, especially through mobile phones, new online consumers are being created. When this is combined with the 2020 pandemic, ecommerce grew by 42%, something that had never happened for at least 15 years. Globally, the ecommerce industry jumped higher by 27%, which was the second-highest growth in the previous 15 years.

What's even more exciting is the ecommerce industry has grown by two digits between 2015 and 2021. There are no signs of this kind of growth slowing down. Ecommerce sales are expected to escalate to 24% of total global retail sales by 2026, which is a growth of 21.8% compared to the 2022 sales. It follows that going into this industry will be one of the best decisions you'll ever make for yourself and your family.

The history of the PoD industry provides further evidence that this market is here to stay. There are signs that the PoD industry existed in China in the third century. Nine centuries later, printing on textiles became popular in Europe. One area where PoD became popular was printing books, something that's still happening today.

In the 1960s, Michael Vasilantone, inventor and artist, invented a new method for screen printing. For the first time, it became many times easier to produce customized designs. Even then, it was still challenging to produce unique designs for the public. This changed in the 1980s when printing on paper became available to the public and PoD began to thrive.

It wasn't until after the invention of the direct-to-garment (DTG) printing method. This allowed printing on fabric. Sensing the opportunity to make money, numerous brands started offering DTG PoD services. If you wanted a personalized pillowcase, you'd order your product and get it produced and delivered. A decade or so later, many more brands competed for a piece of the DTG printing cake.

Over the years, printing technology has advanced. At the same time, the ecommerce industry was growing, which has led to the founding of powerful e-retail giants such as Amazon, Etsy, and eBay. This twin growth—technology advancement and ecommerce growth—combined with the desire for many people to venture into entrepreneurship, has seen the PoD industry growing in leaps and bounds. You can have yourself a share of this growing PoD industry, which is where this book comes in.

If you're looking for a step-by-step guide, this is the book for you. When you're done reading it and implementing the steps and guidance it provides, you'll make thousands of dollars annually. Moreover, you could replace your nine-to-five income and go to business full-time if you wish. In the process, you'll have more free time because you can get others to do most of the work for you.

Starting anything begins with setting the proper foundation. The reason is simple. A weak foundation can't support a gigantic structure, which is what a proper large PoD business is. This is where Chapter 1 of this guide comes in handy when starting a PoD business. What you'll learn in this chapter is what PoD is in more detail and its mechanics. Additionally, you'll learn what makes this business model attractive, especially to people who don't have thousands of savings and a lot of free time. For a balanced view, we also include the disadvantages of PoD to help you make an informed decision, whether this business model is for you or not.

Don't rush to make a decision until after you've read about how a PoD business model works on Amazon and Etsy. We also provide two examples of PoD platforms and their advantages and disadvantages.

When you feel confident that the PoD industry is for you, where do you start? The answer to that question is in Chapter 2. Many beginners make a costly mistake that prevents them from ever trying to run their own business: They start by rushing to create a product they like. Sadly, they're shocked to discover that no one buys their product. Their savings go down the drain and are never to be seen again.

You'll learn in Chapter 2 how to start your business the right way, step-by-step. We suggest that as you read Chapter 2, you implement what you learn, even if it takes you longer to complete reading this chapter. It's that important.

When you've completed the step discussed in Chapter 2, you'll be ready to learn how to find a product to sell. Before searching for a product idea, you need to be clear about the kind of product that appeals to your identified buyer. Once you know the kind of products that appeal to your target buyer, it's time to look for that ideal one. It's crucial that you find a product that not only resonates with your target buyer but also sells. That's why we show you specific places where you can find best-selling products.

Once you have identified the product to sell, you can look for a supplier. Everything you need to complete this step is covered in Chapter 3. Since some product suppliers also offer fulfillment services, we take you through the process of outsourcing to an order fulfillment company.

In Chapter 4, you discover how to market and sell your product. When you're done reading this chapter, you'll understand the customer journey and its importance. For instance, the way you talk with a potential customer ready to buy is different from talking with another one who has no clue that they want your product.

The other crucial element of marketing you'll learn is how to come up with a content marketing strategy. It's not just a matter of throwing content out there and hoping it'll attract customers. There's a strategy behind creating and distributing content that brings people to your brand and converts them into customers.

What happens once your marketing brings customers to your business? If you've done your marketing the right way, people who visit your online store should buy. Know that not all of them will buy for a wide variety of reasons. At any rate, when a customer buys, they expect to receive their order on time. Chapter 5 goes into detail about order fulfillment. When your customers receive their products on time, they'll be happy.

However, there will be times when your order fulfillment operations don't go as planned. It's here where you'll need to know how to address those problems quickly. This chapter will guide you on how to do this and also to optimize your order fulfillment processes.

Your marketing will bring orders together with money. Order fulfillment also costs money. This inflow and outflow of money is a part of the operation of any business. To succeed, a business' outflowing money should not be more than the inflowing. The way to achieve this state of business affairs is through proper financial management and planning.

Don't worry, you don't need to have an accounting degree or master of administration (MBA) degree to manage business finances. Today, there are technological tools that make financial planning and management relatively simple.

Chapter 6 will introduce everything you need about business finances, including the three fundamental financial statements. You'll learn how each is prepared, which will help you learn how to use them. Once you know these financial statements, you'll discover how to make business financial projections.

At this point, you would have created a successful PoD business—a business that generates profit and has money in the bank. Perhaps you might want to expand your business to another level. If so, Chapter 7 is for you. In it, you learn about one vital aspect to have in place before scaling your business. Failing to do this will leave you time-poor and struggling to enjoy life. Once you've implemented this idea, you'll be ready to do the things suggested thereafter, including expanding your product line.

As we said, this book is not only full of information needed to start a PoD business but also provides steps to complete the needed actions. By the time you finish reading and implementing the steps, you'll know how to have a fully functional PoD business. Your total income, personal plus business, will become higher than before you start your business. To have a chance of enjoying this benefit and more, move over to Chapter 1 and start building your business.

Chapter 1:

Getting Started With PoD

PoD allows you to cut a piece of the growing ecommerce industry's cake for yourself without the worries of conventional business. The challenge is that it won't work for you unless you understand the business model and know how to make it work.

In this chapter, you'll discover what PoD is about, how it works, and the different types of this business model that are available. Without further ado, let's jump right into it.

What Is PoD, and How Does It Work?

What comes to mind when you hear "print on demand" or PoD? For many, they start thinking about T-shirts or book self-publishing. Well, PoD covers these and many more. Specifically, PoD is a business model that often runs online.

A PoD business enables you to design, create, market, and sell custom products without keeping finished-product inventory or fulfilling orders. As soon as you sell a product, your white-label product gets printed, packaged, and delivered to your customer by a third party. You can think about a PoD as a dropshipping type of business.

While you can start a PoD business, there are other uses for this model if you already own a company or have a large following. For instance, you can use the PoD approach to:

- **Monetize your following.** Are you a content creator with a large following on social media or have many visitors to your blog? If so, you can make money from those people by creating merchandise to sell.

- **Create promotional products.** Trade shows, conferences, and other types of business events provide a great opportunity to promote your products. By giving people interested in your business an item that features your brand, you can spread the word about your company cheaper. Some of the promotional products you can make include pens, journals, computer mouses, tote bags, keyholders, and many more.

- **Test a new business idea.** Since a PoD company doesn't require you to hold inventory, it's cheaper than a traditional business. This means that you can test different product ideas with next to no financial risk.

There are a few simpler ways of starting a business that are better than PoD. All it takes is finding a third-party supplier of white-label products, customizing them, and selling them. A good example of a white-label product is a mug. You can brand it any way you like and start selling it relatively quickly. There's no need to source the raw materials and manufacture products yourself. All this is often accomplished by third parties if you choose this path.

Your third-party supplier doesn't create a single product unless a customer has already ordered from you. Once a customer places an order, information flows to this supplier, they create the product, and deliver it to your customer. Not only does this approach prevent waste, but it also leaves you with ample time to focus on promoting your business and products. This means that if you can automate your marketing and selling, you can run your business almost hands-free.

The Advantages and Disadvantages of a PoD Business

Like any kind of business model, PoD offers attractive pros while it presents some cons to manage. It's worth knowing in full how this business model will benefit you and what challenges you'll need to overcome to make it work for you. Let's start with its advantages.

Advantages of a PoD Business

- **You don't purchase product manufacturing equipment, which saves you a ton of money in upfront costs**. Your product maker takes care of this. Additionally, you don't need a warehouse to store inventory because you don't require stock. As a result, there's no need for you to manage inventory or hire employees to do these tasks.

- **It's quick to create products once you've submitted your design.** Your manufacturer gets to produce your product as soon as they receive your design. To speed up creating your designs, some platforms provide mockups.

- **There's no need to purchase products in bulk, meaning that you only need a small investment.** A low investment means that you get a higher return on investment (ROI). For instance, if you invest $14 on a white-label product to get to the hands of a customer, and they pay $26 for it, your ROI will be 85.71% (($26 – $14)/$14 = .8571 x 100 = 85.71%). How many businesses can you think of that deliver such an ROI? The profit margin of your business will be 46.15% (($26 – $14)/$26 = .4615 x 100 = 46.15%).

- **You can sell a large selection of products.** If you manufacture your own product, not only will your costs be high, but you'll also be limited in how many types of products you can market and sell. In contrast, PoD offers numerous product types whether clothing, home decor, or accessories. This allows you to sell to a broad audience, like grocers or retailers like Walmart and Best Buy do.

- **A great business model for beginners.** You don't need any form of business experience or know how to run manufacturing operations. Moreover, you don't have to be an expert on shipping or packaging. A fulfilling company will handle these tasks for you, making a PoD easy to start.

Disadvantages of a PoD Business

- **There may be limitations regarding customizations and product options, as these depend on suppliers.** You can overcome this limitation by choosing a platform that offers a large selection of products and customization.

- **It can be hard to handle customer queries because of the split in responsibility between your business and your PoD supplier.** For instance, your supplier may deliver a defective product, and you may have to handle the inevitable customer query. Building a great relationship with your PoD supplier is critical to seamlessly handling issues like this. This again emphasizes how crucial it is to choose a good PoD company.

- **It takes longer to ship the product to a customer compared to traditional retailers.** While this is true, you have a duty to convince customers that they're not buying a run-of-the-mill product, but a unique product that can't be found at traditional retailers.

- **Product cost per item is higher than in bulk-produced items.** This will lower your profit margin. However, this doesn't mean that you won't get a good profit margin. It's just that it'll be lower than if similar products were mass-produced.

- **You have limited control over your customer's boxing experience and shipping costs.** However, you can collaborate with your PoD supplier to make sure that you wow your customers so that they can buy again.

As you can see, there are ways to work around the limitations of a PoD business when you can have influence. This is great because you can have an added influence on your customers and get them to buy more and more often, which is great for making tons of dollars.

How Does a PoD Company Differ From a Regular Dropshipping Business?

We mentioned above that PoD is a subset of traditional dropshipping. In both of these, a customer orders from you, and a third-party supplier takes care of the rest: production, packaging, and shipping.

There are important differences between the PoD model and dropshipping you should know. While PoD kicks in once a customer has purchased a product, dropshipping manufactures products in bulk. As a result, dropshipping delivers products faster because there's no production once the customer has placed their order. All it takes is packaging the product and delivering it. In contrast, production in PoD slows down the pace at which you will receive your product. This is the price customers pay for wanting custom products.

PoD Print Types

Printing is one of the major jobs your PoD supplier will do for you. How will you want them to print your products? That's a tough question to answer if you aren't familiar with the different PoD print types. This part of the book lists and describes each of the ways you can print your items. This information will enable you to choose one that's fit for you and your customer's printing needs, whether it's the appearance or practicality. For your business, speed of production and print performance may be more important.

Vinyl Printing

Have you seen those shirts with printing that feels like plastic? The printing type used to create such print is called vinyl printing. The print doesn't get absorbed into the fabric but sits on top of it. This printing process begins with printing your design on heat transfer paper. This is followed by transferring the design onto a garment by using heat coupled with pressure.

It's a great print type for a smaller volume of material because it's inexpensive. Vinyl printing's weakness is that it is time-consuming just to produce one print. For instance, you have to manually trim back the transfer paper. As a result, it's not ideal for large PoD jobs. Customers may not like it because the print can crack or fade over time.

DTG Printing

DTG is like printing material with a mammoth LaserJet printer. This means that it prints by spraying ink onto a garment. Unlike vinyl printing, the ink percolates into the fabric. It was created for mass-production garment printing. It works great on 100% cotton, but can be used on other materials that blend cotton with other types of fabrics.

The biggest advantages of DTG printing are that it's inexpensive, quick, works with various colors, and prints in great detail. However, it lacks consistency when printing from one garment to the next. This means that you can have a perfect print on a burgundy T-shirt but imperfect on a royal blue one. The other disadvantage is that DTG printing doesn't work well on other types of fabrics without cotton.

Embroidery

Embroidery isn't printing, but the process of sewing a design onto a material. It's the old-school method of having prints on garments. Today, there are embroidery machines that allow faster printing production. Here's how the modern embroidery method works.

You produce a design you want on your material. This design gets converted into a digital embroidery file that traces the placement and color of every stitch. You then load this file onto an embroidery machine having spools of thread needed for the design colors.

The good news is that "printing" produced this way is durable and has a high perceived value. Most importantly, you get consistent colors from one garment to the next. You can charge higher prices for your products than in any other printing method.

As you probably guessed, this form of garment "printing" is time-consuming and, therefore, expensive compared to other printing methods. This method is also not ideal for complex designs.

Digisoft

If you want a print type that delivers low error rates, enhanced print longevity, and consistent color, Digisoft is your ideal choice. This is a proprietary print technology that produces high-quality printing on various kinds of fabrics. It works a lot like direct-to-film (DTF) printing we'll discuss shortly. Not only does this process print at scale, but it's also precise and versatile.

Some printing types produce prints that crack or peel because they're inflexible. Such is not the case with Digisoft, as the prints move synchronously with the fabric.

While Digisoft prints both simple and complex designs, it may not be a preferred choice for distressed designs.

Sublimation Printing

Do you remember what the term "sublimation" means from your high school science class? If you do, that's great. In case you may have forgotten, sublimation means turning a solid directly into a gas. For instance, exposing dry ice (frozen carbon dioxide) turns it into gas. This technique can be used to print on various types of materials, whether porous or hard surfaces.

For garments, sublimation printing works well on white polyester materials. Instead of printing a graphic tee, this method suits printing the entire garment. You need to place the garnet flat for color consistency across the whole garment. Failure to do this is the main cause of higher error rates and waste. Because it prints seam to seam, it delivers great longevity and accurate color.

DTF Printing

If you want to produce more durable printing than you can get with DTG, DTF printing is your go-to print type. DTF came into the PoD scene in 2021. It produces more vibrant colors and prints DTG.

DTF printing uses a heat-press machine to bind a design or image onto a garment. But first, you print the image or design onto a special film and cover it with an adhesive setting powder. You allow the film to cure, place it onto your garment, and press it with the heat-press machine.

While DTF is great for decorating fabrics, it suffers from a lack of scalability. The reason is that the powdering and pressing processes are manual. However, if getting long-lasting and vibrant colors is more important, this type of printing suits you.

Screen Printing

Screen printing has stood the test of time for more than 1,000 years. It derives its name from the way it works. The method pushes one-colored ink through silk screens onto a garment. To get multiple colors to the garment, you need to push the ink one color at a time. Each color uses a custom-made screen, making it expensive for small print runs.

The print produced feels great in your hands, the colors are vibrant and durable. For simpler designs, screen printing produces wonderful prints cost-effectively for large orders. Its weakness is that it doesn't produce good prints for complex designs such as the ones in photographic prints. Moreover, the more colors there are in your designs, the more expensive it will be to print.

At the end of the day, the choice of print type will depend largely on your needs, including the type of print, the material you print on, and the quality of the print. However, you should choose a printing method that delivers the quality that your customers want. Otherwise, you'll struggle to get them to buy more and buy more often. If that happens, your business will not scale, and that is a tragedy in the world of business.

Should You Partner With a PoD Platform or Service Provider?

We trust that by now you have a good understanding of how a PoD works. You need to have a product you want to sell and partner with a PoD company to ensure your product reaches your customer. There are two kinds of partner companies to choose from: platforms like Etsy and Amazon, or service providers such as Printful and Printify.

In this section, we'll look at how working with a platform differs from partnering with a service provider. Specifically, we'll look at how Etsy and Amazon work in relation to PoD, their pros and cons, and how Printful and Printify work, including their pros and cons. When we're finished, you should be able to decide which one is best for you.

How Etsy and Amazon PoD Work in the PoD Industry

Etsy and Amazon are two of the giants of the ecommerce industry. Both are great marketplaces where business owners list and sell their products. They differ in how they work when it comes to PoD. Etsy offers merchants a platform to make PoD sales while Amazon provides more. Since these two companies could be your PoD partner, it's worth understanding how each works and how it can benefit your PoD business.

Etsy is known as a marketplace for handmade items, crafts, and vintage goods. This has changed in recent times. Now, the company hosts numerous online stores that sell clothing, accessories, and many other items. This suggests that your type of customer visits Etsy looking for certain products.

Etsy's website welcomed 377.4 million visitors in June 2022. Of this traffic, 58.79% comes from the US. It's exciting that sales of merchandise on Etsy have been increasing. For instance, sales grew from $10.2 billion in 2020 to $13.5 billion in 2021. Astonishingly, Etsy sales have more than doubled between 2019 and 2021, which is an exciting story. What does this mean for you as a PoD business owner? You can make money on Etsy if you know how, which is why you should keep reading.

Etsy debuted in the ecommerce space in 2005. It's a marketplace where business owners list their products for sale to their target customers. In this way, it doesn't differ from eBay or Redbubble. This means that Etsy doesn't create PoD products. However, you can get these products elsewhere (discussed below) and list them for sale on Etsy.

You'll still benefit from third-party customization, production, packaging, and shipping of your products to customers. This is what you'll need to do before selling your PoD products on Etsy:

1. **Find a PoD niche represented on Etsy.** A niche is a subset of a given market. For instance, sun care is a niche within the larger skincare industry. A niche allows you to laser-target your customers and potentially sell your products at a premium. We'll discuss the subject of choosing a niche later.

2. **Locate a trusted Etsy PoD manufacturer.** There are numerous PoD product manufacturers and this can make finding the right partner challenging. Finding a good fit is like hiring a new employee. Imagine that you're hiring an employee to take care of printing and fulfilling orders for your PoD products! What qualities would you want that employee to

have? We have no doubt that you'll want a trustworthy, honest, hard-working, and caring employee. Your PoD manufacturer should tick similar boxes as well. Finding the best manufacturing PoD partner requires thorough research and vetting. Make sure that your chosen PoD manufacturer offers the products you want to sell.

Once you've found the right niche and PoD manufacturer, it's time to list and sell your products on Etsy.

Selling Your PoD Products on Etsy

If you think Etsy is the right marketplace to sell your PoD products, you need to take steps to list your products. Here's how the listing steps work.

1. **Create an Etsy account.** Go to etsy.com/sell and click or tap the "get started" button. You'll be given the option to sign up with your Google, Facebook, or Apple account. Choose one that applies to you and follow the instructions that come up. Etsy might ask you a few questions before you get the option to start your online store.

2. **Set up your Etsy store.** Once you hit the "start shop" button, you'll be taken to a page where you can fill in the details of your shop. Here's what you'll need to fill in:

    a. **Shop language:** The language Etsy uses to describe your products. Once selected, you can't change it later. However, you can add other languages later.

    b. **Shop country:** This is the country from which you'll operate your store.

    c. **Shop currency:** The currency used to price your PoD products. When an international customer visits your store, they'll see prices in their local currency. When done, hit the save and continue button.

3. **Name your Etsy online store.** Etsy requires merchants to use unique names for their online stores. The name you choose should have 4 to 20 characters, have no space or special characters, and doesn't violate any trademark. Most importantly, use a name that is easy to understand and remember and indicates what your brand is about. Immediately you enter a store name, Etsy will check its availability. If someone already uses the name, Etsy will suggest alternatives.

4. **List your PoD products.** This is arguably an exciting stage for many PoD business owners. You've worked hard to find a PoD partner, and you're now about to sell your products. You first need to list your products, which is like stocking items on store shelves in a physical retail store. Here are the main elements involved in listing a product on Etsy:

   a. **Add clear photos and a video.** Online customers rely on product photos and a video to make buying decisions. Simplify this for your customers by providing great product photos from different angles as well as a video, if need be. Etsy's guidelines and best practices will help you get this right.

   b. **Select your product's thumbnail image.** By default, your product thumbnail is the first image you uploaded in the previous step. However, you can change it so that you can have the best photo on product search results.

   c. **Write product listing details.** An image alone isn't enough to mussell successfully online. You need additional information about your product such as its name, the category it belongs to, and what the product is about. Etsy allows you to enter this information in the "add listing details" section.

d. Describe your product. Customers rely a lot on product descriptions. You need to clearly describe what the product does for the customer. Avoid simply telling customers what the product is because they're more interested in how they'll benefit if they bought the product. This applies to both physical and digital products. Note that your description influences how high your product will be listed when customers search for similar products.

5. **Add PoD production partners.** Do you remember we earlier mentioned that you should first find a PoD partner before opening an Etsy store? It was to make this step easier and quicker. On the product listing page, you'll see the Production Partners section that takes you through the process of adding a PoD partner. The information to add includes the following:

    a. Production partner name: Type the name of your PoD partner. If you don't want your customers to know who this is, use the toggle provided and choose to add a descriptive title.

    b. Location: State where your PoD partner is based.

    c. About your partnership with your PoD partner: You need to give details about your and your partner's role. For instance, you need to mention why you chose this partner, what your role in the design process is, and what your partner does in the production process. When finished, save the partner.

6. **Finalize your PoD Etsy store settings.** The last step of setting up your Etsy store is to set up Etsy payments, subscription billing options, and shop customizations. Follow the onscreen instructions to complete these last actions. When finished, your store will be ready to serve your customers. Remember that people won't go to your store unless they know

that it exists. It's your job to make sure that you send them to your store and not rely on customers that visit Etsy. Otherwise, your business will succeed by chance, which is not how to build any thriving business.

What Fees Does Etsy Charge?

We mentioned above that one of the factors to consider when choosing a PoD platform or service provider is pricing. The price you pay contributes hugely to your profit margin. The lower the price you can get, the higher your profit margin will be. With that in mind, let's explore the fees that Etsy charges so that you can determine if this platform suits you or not.

1. **Listing fees:** Etsy charges a fee when you list a product for the first time or renew it. For each item you list, you'll pay $0.20, which is also the case even when you list multiple quantities of a particular product. Any Etsy listing gets automatically renewed after 4 months. However, you can set the renewal to manual if you wish.

2. **Transaction fees:** A transaction occurs when a customer buys your product. Etsy charges a fee called a transaction cost at 6.5% of the purchase price of the item. For instance, if the item price is $20, Etsy will charge a transaction fee of $1.30 ($20 x 6.5% = $20 x .065 = $1.30).

3. **Payment processing fees:** If you use the Etsy Payments system, Etsy will charge you a payment processing fee. The amount charged consists of a fixed portion and a variable part that depends on the sales price of your item.

The above are the main Etsy fees for a regular Etsy subscription. There may be other fees if you advertise on this platform or opt for the Etsy Plus subscription.

The individual costs associated with your Etsy store may seem small, but they can add to a big sum quickly. You need to figure out what their impact on your profit margin will be.

Etsy PoD Pros and Cons

Pros

- **Access to traffic:** Etsy has nearly 90 million active buyers and ranks 4th behind Apple in terms of growth. Because of this access to traffic, you may spend less on advertising costs to acquire customers.

- **Products have high perceived values:** Products on Etsy enjoy exclusivity due to the positioning of the platform as a marketplace for independent designers. Thus, similar items sold anywhere else are likely to cost less than on Etsy, which can bring better profit margins.

- **Provides a good buying mood for PoD customers:** Customers visit Etsy to buy custom products. This augurs well for PoD products because they're unique and more personalized.

Cons

- **High competition:** Having millions of buyers on Etsy is a good thing. However, it also attracts a lot of sellers, which increases your competition and makes it difficult to stand out. You can work around this challenge by developing and executing an effective marketing strategy. We'll cover marketing and sales later because of their importance for any PoD business.

- **Price drive down:** What happens when the competition is high in any niche on Etsy or any other platform? Some competitors gravitate to dropping the prices of their merchandise. You then will have a hard time keeping your prices high and generating higher profit margins. This means you need to position your PoD business differently so that you don't compete on price but on value.

- **It's challenging to build brand loyalty:** Imagine that a customer buys your beautiful product on Etsy. A friend visits them and sees the product, and asks, *"Where did you purchase that from?"* the likely answer is, "I bought it from Etsy." Sadly, Etsy isn't the name of your business, meaning that your brand may not grow as much as you want on this platform. You'll need to think about methods to promote the image of your business, including perhaps using branded packaging and communicating regularly with your customers via tools such as email.

If you would like to learn more about running your own successful Etsy store, why not take a look at our book, ***Etsy Store Mastery: The Ultimate Guide to Building Your Own Etsy Empire***?

How Amazon PoD Works

If Etsy doesn't sound like a good fit for your PoD business, an alternative platform you can use is Amazon—the king of ecommerce globally. It's exciting to note that 67% of online buyers go to Amazon to check the prices of the items of their interest. There are nearly 9 in 10 online shoppers who would rather buy from Amazon than any other ecommerce website.

Buyers go to Amazon to purchase many kinds of products, including gowns, mugs, cups, stationery, electronics, and T-shirts. This is great for someone interested in starting a PoD business.

There are two ways of doing PoD business on Amazon. The first is by using a platform called Amazon Merch on Demand, while the second works like that of Etsy and is termed an Amazon seller account. The option we'd like to dig deeper into is Amazon Merch on Demand. Merch on Demand allows you to create designs, print them on a variety of items, and sell the resulting products.

Unlike Etsy, you earn royalties for your designs after Amazon has taken its cut for materials, labor, shipping, and other production costs. The good news is that you set the price for your merchandise.

The second method requires you to have a professional Amazon seller account—you can subscribe to for $39.99 a month. Of course, there are additional selling fees that you may have to pay.

The option we'd like to dig deeper into is the second one. The reason is that Amazon Merch on Demand has a high demand, and you can only access it by invitation only. It might not be easy to access this platform as a beginner.

Steps to Sell Amazon PoD Products

The following five steps simplify how to sell your PoD products on Amazon and access the millions upon millions of people who visit this giant website. Like Etsy, you need to first figure out which PoD manufacturer to work with before you can start selling your products on Amazon. Make sure that you have opened an account with your PoD product supplier before following the steps below.

- **Step 1: Register for an Amazon account:** This step applies if you don't already have an Amazon account. Simply head over to amazon.com and click on the sign-in option in the top-right corner of the screen. You'll get an option to open an account as a new customer.

- **Step 2: Create an Amazon seller account:** If you don't have an Amazon seller account, create one by visiting sell.amazon.com/. Otherwise, if you have a seller account, log into it.

- **Step 3: Create your product designs in your PoD supplier's account:** A good PoD manufacturer will have a drag-and-drop feature to help simplify the creation of your product designs. Use this to create your designs and where they need to be positioned on your products. Also, specify what type of printing you want to use. Remember to have various views of your product for effective listing on Amazon.

- **Step 4: Connect your PoD manufacturer with Amazon:** How fast this happens will depend on whether your PoD manufacturer integrates directly with Amazon or not. A PoD supplier like Printful requires that you apply for a GTIN exemption from Amazon to avoid buying barcodes from this giant ecommerce company. Don't worry, this often occurs quickly. Once you've connected your PoD manufacturer, your products will be listed on Amazon.

- **Step 5: Optimize your product listing:** This is where you need to use keywords to describe your products. This will make it easier for Amazon to find it when someone searches for a similar product. Use keywords in the names of your products and their descriptions. Focus more on what the product does for the customers than on what it is.

Amazon PoD Pros and Cons

Pros

- Amazon allows you to use your designs wherever you choose. This means you can sell your PoD products on other ecommerce websites without worrying about lawsuits.

- You have access to numerous Amazon website visitors, presenting you with a wide customer base. This helps keep your marketing and advertising budget low, which can push your profit margins higher.

Cons

- Amazon charges a referral fee, meaning that you pay for acquiring customers from its platform. When adding these fees to the monthly subscription and sales commission, your profit margins can turn out to be low.

- You face intense seller competition. The higher number of Amazon visitors attracts too much seller competition, the same way as a school of salmon attracts sharks. This may force you to lower your prices if your competitor undercuts you. You'll need to have strategies to appear more valuable to your customers than your competitors.

How Printful and Printify Work in the PoD Industry

Whether you're selling on Etsy, Amazon, or any other ecommerce website, you'll need a partner to create your products and fulfill customer orders. It's crucial to choose a suitable PoD manufacturer for one important reason: Your PoD supplier will interact with your customers and influence their experiences. This will play a huge role in whether these customers continue to buy from you or not. Moreover, you want a reliable supplier.

Although there are numerous PoD suppliers, two of the popular ones are Printful and Printify. Let's look at what each is and how it works so that you can make an informed PoD supplier choice.

Printful and How It Works

Printful is a PoD supplier founded in 2013 by businessman Lauris Liberts. This company now has 14 printing and fulfillment centers. Amazingly, Printful delivers at least 1 million items each month for its PoD business partners.

One of this platform's exciting features is that it integrates with some of the best ecommerce websites in the world, including Amazon, Shopify, Etsy, and Squarespace. This means that you can take advantage of organic traffic that visits these behemoths of the ecommerce industry. We like the fact that Printful can also fulfill orders for products that you source elsewhere.

When a customer purchases your product, the order automatically filters to Printful for fulfillment. As a result, you don't need to keep any inventory or pay any fees, except when a customer places an order. However, since you'd already have the money, your customer technically pays the costs associated with their order.

Product design is simple on Printful. You get access to an online mockup generator to create your desired products. This means you can create products with minimal design skills. Furthermore, Printful has a wide array of products you can sell, such as clothing and home products.

To use Printful, you have to link it with your online store. That's why it is far easier to first create your online store before integrating it with Printful. You can open an online store with a variety of ecommerce platforms that support Printful, including eBay, Amazon, Etsy, Shopify, and WooCommerce. How you link Printful with any of these platforms varies. Others can integrate with Printful directly and automatically, while others require manual linking.

Advantages of Printful

- It's user-friendly even for beginners. Whether you want to create mockups and products or integrate Printful with ecommerce platforms, it's intuitive to do so. The learning curve is low.

- It offers generous discounts for more than 1,000 sales per month. It's not unheard of to get between 5% and 9% in discounts. This means that if you're normally charged $10 per order, you can pay as little as $9.10 ($10 x $(100 - 9)/100 = $9.10). Speaking about costs, you don't pay any monthly or setup fees to list your products on Printful.

- Printful manufactures high product quality. Not only does this company provide various printing techniques, but it also sources quality materials. It achieves this by partnering with top suppliers.

- It integrates with more than 20 ecommerce platforms. This means that you have a wider selection of ecommerce platforms to choose from. As a result, you can opt for cheaper platforms, bringing your overall operational costs down and improving your profit margins.

- You can sell to customers in more than 170 countries. This is made possible by Printful's global network of manufacturing and fulfillment centers. You can ship products faster and cheaper because of the proximity of Printful facilities to your customers.

Disadvantages of Printful

- It doesn't have as extensive a product catalog as some big names in the PoD industry, such as Printify.

- You may be charged additional fees depending on the design you want on your products. For instance, you may like a certain premium photo thinking it's free but be charged a certain fee.

- Its technical support could be better. The reason is that it doesn't offer phone support, meaning that delays in resolving issues can happen.

Printify and How It Works

One of the exciting alternatives to Printful is Printify, a company cofounded by businesspeople James Berdigans, Artis Kehris, and Gatis Dukurs in 2015. If you're looking for a PoD service provider with a wide range of products, Printify is your great option.

This PoD company differs from Printful in that it's more of a middle person than a PoD product manufacturer. What it does is bring together PoD businesses with PoD product manufacturers. It's these PoD manufacturers that handle the creation, packaging, and delivery of your products to your customers. This business model allows it to scale much faster than competitors like Printful.

Printify works very much the same as Printful. When a customer orders a product, Printify charges your bank account for manufacturing, printing, and delivery costs. How long it takes before you receive the money from your customer will depend on your bank's policy. However, Printify charges your bank account immediately, meaning that you should always have money in your account.

The quality of the products you get from Printify varies based on manufacturers. It's helpful to research the manufacturer you choose to use to ensure that you sell quality products. Perhaps you should consider ordering a sample each from several manufacturers before listing them in your online store.

Advantages of Printify

- It offers 24/7 support.

- It provides template product descriptions to emulate for your own.

- Printify has more than 800 products, offering variety.

- It boasts a diverse group of PoD manufacturers, which offers options regarding quality and cost.

- Choosing a product to list is easy.

Disadvantages of Printify

- It offers fewer integrations to ecommerce websites compared to alternatives like Printful.

- Printify doesn't accept modification of its in-house packaging material. For instance, you can't add a logo to its packaging.

- You need to sign up for a paid subscription plan to access generous discounts.

It's clear that a PoD business is a great way to start your entrepreneurial journey. You don't need to have large sums of upfront costs to pay. This is great because you can get a better ROI for your money.

You need to do thorough research when choosing an online store and a PoD service provider. Don't forget to opt for partners that will allow your business to scale as the years wear on.

If you're convinced that starting a PoD business is the way to go, you need to do what's discussed in the next chapter. But first, complete the following checklist before moving to the next chapter. Opening accounts on PoD platforms and ecommerce marketplaces gives you a chance to practice what you've learned. You might also make up your mind about which platforms to use.

To ensure that you take steps to start your PoD business, mark on the left side column all the tasks you've completed.

Checklist

	Create a Printify or Printful account. Follow the guidelines to select a product and create a design.
	Open an Etsy account and create your online store. It doesn't have to be perfect as the aim is to learn PoD skills.
	Connect your product supplier (Printify or Printful) account to your Etsy online store.
	Decide on the kind of printing you want to use on your PoD product

Chapter 2:

Finding Your Niche and Business

Branding

You probably began thinking about some PoD business ideas while reading the previous chapter. That's great. Beginner business owners tend to want to sell their products or services to everyone. Unfortunately, this doesn't work, for reasons you'll know shortly. What you want is to target a niche—a part of a larger market introduced in Chapter 1.

How do you find such a niche? Most importantly, what is a niche, and why should businesses choose them instead of macro markets? This chapter answers those questions and also shows you how to brand your business.

Defining Your Niche and Why You Need It

Imagine that a baseball player gets hit in the eye by a baseball. Unfortunately, they suffer serious eye injuries. Who do you think this player should be taken to between a general practitioner and an ophthalmologist? Of course, the player should be sent to an ophthalmologist because this doctor handles complex eye issues and performs surgery. A general practitioner will probably refer the player to an eye medical doctor.

The general practitioner deals with all kinds of diseases but doesn't have special knowledge about any of them. This doctor is like the general market that you may target as a PoD business owner. In contrast, an ophthalmologist is a specialist doctor whose target market is eye patients. These medical doctors charge a lot more than general practitioners to treat eye problems. In this illustration, eye care is a niche within the healthcare industry. Do you now get what it means by a business niche?

A niche is a small section of a broader market. For instance, selling T-shirts for seniors is a niche within the clothing industry. As you can see, you get to know who your target market is within a niche. However, that isn't the case in a wider market.

If you try to sell every product in the PoD industry, your focus will be scattered; you won't have the resources to run an effective PoD business. It's far better and easier to operate a targeted PoD business.

The Benefits of Targeting a Niche in Business

Do you remember why people prefer buying PoD products? They buy because of the uniqueness of the products. Finding a niche makes it easier to create such products.

There are many more advantages when you focus on a niche, including the following:

- **A niche leads to cheaper marketing expenses.** When you market to a group of people whom you know their pains and desires better than they do, you get better responses. You target your advertisements better. Your target audience feels that you know them and their needs, which makes it easier to build relationships with them. In business and life, money comes from good relationships. Additionally, because you target a small group of people, it will be cheaper to reach them.

- **It helps build loyalty with your customers.** The biggest marketing expense for most businesses is the customer acquisition cost (CAC). Think of CAC as the amount of money you spend to acquire a single customer. It makes sense to keep a customer for as long as possible so that you can reclaim this cost and even gain profit. You can't keep customers for long if you don't know them well and haven't built good relationships with them. A niche helps you build these relationships because you know your customers better than anyone. As a result, you can deliver unrivaled customer service, which leads to creating long-term customers.

- **A niche increases business profitability.** The way to increase profits is by lowering costs. This is where a lower CAC comes in handy, but that's not all. You can also charge higher prices than generic competitors for the same products. Do you remember how ophthalmologists' prices differ from those of general practitioners? The specialist—who targets a niche—charges higher prices. With higher prices at the same costs, you'll generate improved profits.

- **It differentiates your business from the competition.** While competition is great, it can also lead to lower sales. This is particularly true when you sell generic products that can be found in many other stores. A niche instantly makes your business different from your competition. Imagine a 7-ft person standing among a group of 4-ft to 5-ft people! There's no doubt you'll be able to spot that person from miles away. That will be like your PoD business if you go into a particular niche. It will stand out, and people will easily find it.

- **A niche allows you to become an authority.** Do you sometimes listen to podcasts, talk radio, or conversation-rich TV programs? Or, do you pay attention to instructions and messages coming from the U.S. Capitol Complex? Podcasts and talk radio usually involve authorities on topics under discussion. Who doesn't pay attention to news from Congress? The reason we pay attention is that authority accompanies that news. When you're an expert in your field, people listen to what you say. Many go on to do what you tell them to do. It is not a mistake that expert marketers instruct their target audience to act in a certain way.

With such benefits of having a niche, you can't afford to not find one for your PoD business. The question is how to go about doing so, and the answer is below.

Five Steps to Finding a Niche

It's now time to get your hands dirty to find a niche you'd enjoy doing business in. When you combine your niche with your passions, you instantly become an expert in your field. Do you remember the benefit of being an authority? If you aren't at that authority level yet, getting there will be quick.

Finding a PoD business niche is a six-step process to be followed in the sequence below. Let's dive right in.

Step 1: Discover What You're Passionate About

There's one mistake many people make: They separate their passions and work. What does this mean? For many, work is a means to earn income to cater to all their needs and wants. The problem is that a person can spend as much as a third of their life working. Furthermore, most of this time is usually during the day. You can imagine how terrible your days will be if you don't enjoy your work.

The sad news is that at least 20% of U.S. workers aren't passionate about their jobs. It's surprising that about 61% are happy with their jobs, but 61% plan on leaving their jobs. Although these statistics change, you can count on meeting millions of U.S. workers who are not passionate about their jobs.

Going into business will not change a thing unless you choose to do what you're passionate about. Your business should be an extension of your passions so that even when you do business, it doesn't feel like work. That's why the first thing you should do is figure out your passions.

Grab a piece of paper and a pen, or fire up a spreadsheet on your computer, and begin to note down things that you're passionate about. Do you like football, basketball, charity, teaching, fitness and wellness, health, or reading? Make a note of it. Write as many passions as you can think of. You may also explore your passions by checking the kind of YouTube videos that get recommended to you in your YouTube feed. Another potential place is on regular websites that run banner ads. Check the kind of ads you often see.

When you've identified your passions, list them in terms of priority from top to bottom. You'll need this in the next step.

Step 2: Research the Market

You're now going to research the market that corresponds with your passions and interests. It's vital to understand what a market is before going any further.

Economists consider a market as a place where buyers and sellers exchange goods or services with money. This definition is okay in economics, but not for the purpose of finding a business niche. From this view, a market is a group of people with identifiable wants and needs they want to satisfy.

You can use certain words to check if there's a market related to your passions. Let's imagine that your top passion is dogs. You can't know ahead of time what people want to know or say about dogs. Your best bet for finding this out is through doing offline and online searches. Online searching works better because it's fast. With this in mind, let's use Google Trends to figure out what people are searching for about dogs.

All it takes is firing up your browser and entering this address trends.google.com to launch Google Trends. Choose the country and period of interest. In this case, the word of interest is "dog" and you can enter the search trend period by selecting a start date and an end date, and it will show the trends within that specific time period. The search results show the level of interest people have, or had, in dogs during the time you selected. This will be a good niche to pursue if looking for an evergreen topic.

You can scroll down to explore which areas lead on your topics of interest. Further down, you'll find related searches that people are making and topics. You can click on any of the queries or topics to investigate further.

Another great tool to find business niches is Semrush or similar websites such as Ahrefs and SimilarWeb. Putting the word "dog" in Semrush's Keyword Overview tool returns numerous other ideas. Most importantly, you'll find out how many people have an interest in your idea, both in the US and internationally. For instance, there are 1.2 million searches of the word "dog" in the US. Globally, that number jumps to five million. Can you believe that the word dog is used the most in India?

Not only do you now know how popular your keyword is, but you also find other ideas related to your keyword. For instance, one keyword you might like is "Bernese Mountain Dog." You can imagine producing T-shirts adorned with images of a Bernese Mountain Dog!

Don't forget to explore Google when you do your market research. If you're after trends, Trendhunter can be your good friend.

Step 3: Run a Competitor Analysis

You can find an amazingly popular idea and still not make money with it. That would be tragic, wouldn't it? A good PoD business idea should already be making money for others. That's a sign that there are people willing to spend money in that market, which is what you want.

You may feel like it's a good idea to be a pioneer. Well, if you pioneer something, you'll probably be added to historical records. However, it will take a long time before you make money. If you want to make money in a short time and reach your financial goals, your best bet is to analyze your competition before starting your PoD business.

Suppose that one of your passions is to raise awareness about the dangers of diabetes. A keyword search on Semrush shows that many people want to know information and facts about this disease. Most of the search results on Google are for organizations that want to share information about this ailment. Reading at least 10 website pages listed in the search results can give you an idea regarding what type of information people want. Better still, head over to Amazon.com and read reviews of books about diabetes. Take as many notes as you can. The reviewers tell you what they like and don't like about your competitors.

Also, check your competitors' ads to identify what appeals to the customers in your niche. You can find ads on search engines such as Google and Bing and social media platforms, including YouTube, Instagram, and Facebook.

As you study your competitors, you'll discover their strengths and weaknesses. These findings will come in handy when you position your PoD company.

Step 4: Define Your Niche

After you've identified your passions and interests, researched the market for a couple of those passions, and analyzed the competition, you should have found your potential niche. This niche should be profitable—hence, the competition—and fill you with excitement to serve it.

Your next step is to define your niche. When doing so, it should be clear what kind of products appeal to them. For instance, does your niche welcome eco-friendly or handmade products? How about product pricing? Does your niche buy moderately priced products or luxury items? You also need to know a lot about your target buyer, which is where the next step will help you.

Step 5: Define Your Buyer Persona

Who are you going to sell your products in your chosen niche? There's no need to guess the answer because you can find out who your ideal target buyer is. The problem is that you can't target a single person because different people may be equally attracted to your businesses. That's why marketing tools often report audience data in age ranges, such as 25 to 44-year-olds.

You performed market research and analyzed your competition, which gave you an idea about the type of people buying products in your niche. There's much more information you need about your target audience so that you can know who your PoD business will target. The end point of this process will be a buyer persona—a fictional person who has the characteristics of your ideal target buyer.

The first piece of information you need about your audience is their demographics. This involves knowing your target audience's physical location, education level, age range, gender, income level, job title, industry, and marriage status. Demographics alone aren't enough for targeting your ideal buyer. You also need to know their psychographics, which are intangible characteristics of your ideal buyer. These include values, interests, beliefs, lifestyles, and political views.

There's more to know about your ideal target audience. For instance, you need to know who influences them, whether it's Robert Kiyosaki, Tony Robbins, Lisa Nichols, J.K. Rowling, or whomever. Along with this, you also need to know their favorite websites and social media platforms, and preferred media (online or print). Armed with this information, you'll communicate with your audience effectively.

A buyer persona isn't complete without identifying the pain points of your target audience. This is where you need to find out what prevents them, from their point of view, from achieving their dreams. This is crucial because people buy to either solve problems or achieve certain goals. If you can know these goals and challenges, you'll create relevant products that will fly off your store's shelves.

When you're done collecting information about your ideal target audience, it's time to create your buyer persona. To illustrate, let's say that your ideal buyer has the following characteristics:

- Gender: Female

- Age range: 25–34

- Job title: Software developer and employed full-time

- Income level: $80,000–$120,000 (Sources like Glassdoor, Indeed, and PayScale are helpful in finding this out)

- Household size: 3–5

- Education: Bachelor's degree

- Interests: Reading fiction and personal finance books and enjoys watching soccer

- Social media: YouTube and Facebook

Let's now write a story that describes the above target buyer. We'll call the above ideal buyer, Amelia Norton.

Amelia Norton is a female aged 25–34 who lives in Tennessee with her husband and 3 children. She holds a bachelor's degree from the University of Maryland and works full-time for a technology company. When she's not at work, she reads various fiction genres, especially mystery novels, and personal finance books.

From time to time, she hops onto YouTube to catch up with the latest on U.S. soccer. While on YouTube, she checks motivational videos by Tony Robbins or the *Motiveristy* YouTube channel. She also catches up with friends on Facebook twice a week to share her thoughts about the books she reads.

Note that the above story is made-up based on the actual buyer data from various sources such as Semrush, SimilarWeb, and Glassdoor. Of course, there are many more tools you can use for the same purpose.

The endpoint of defining your buyer persona is a visual of your ideal customer. You now know who you're going to be selling to.

Step 6: Run a Second Competitor Analysis

The first competitor analysis you performed helped you identify a niche to go into. This second one focuses on competitors in the niche you have chosen and helps with determining your value proposition, a step discussed next.

Again, tools like Google, Semrush, SimilarWeb, and Ahrefs will come in handy in this research. All it takes is getting great insights on SimilarWeb and Semrush is entering a competitor website address, and you'll receive a ton of vital information. Specifically, you'll learn a lot about your competitor customers.

Additionally, study customer reviews and the products that your competitors offer. Don't forget to gauge your competitors' customer service. At the end of your research, you should know what makes your competitors successful in your niche.

Step 7: Define Your Value Proposition

Why do you think people buy from a particular business over and over again? They get better value for their money than doing business with any other company. For instance, they may be getting never-before-seen customer service or product quality, or a unique product style. It's for this reason that you need to define your value proposition.

A value proposition describes the most important benefit you offer to your target audience. The benefit you offer should be unique and appeal to your perfect customer. Best of all, it should differentiate your PoD business from all your competitors.

The characteristics of a powerful and attractive value proposition consist of three features: It's clear what customer pain it alleviates or what desire it satisfies—it's specific and communicates your exclusiveness.

Your product or its features don't form part of your value proposition. Instead, it communicates an experience that each of your customers feels for doing business with you.

The best way to capture your value proposition is as a statement. Coming up with this statement hinges on understanding your customer and the benefits of your product.

The following three tips will help come up with a potent value proposition:

1. **Use specific benefits and avoid superlatives.** While doing the research mentioned above, you should have thought about the kind of product you'll start with. Whatever that product is, what benefits will it confer on your ideal buyer? Be as concrete as possible without gravitating to using superlatives such as "the best T-shirt in the PoD world." Your buyers have no conception of what it means by "best in the world." However, saying the printing on your T-shirt doesn't crack and the T-shirt material lasts at least 5 years tells your buyer what they'll benefit from buying it.

2. **Use the customer's language in your value proposition statement.** You should find this out when studying the profile of your ideal buyer. Your competitor's customer reviews and testimonials are great fodder for this sort of language. Using this language helps make sure that your target customers see themselves in your value proposition.

3. **Focus on clarity instead of creativity.** It should be clear what major benefit your product delivers and how this will better your customers' lives. Every word you use should be clear and devoid of jargon.

When all is said and done, your value proposition should tell the customer what your product does better than any of its kind.

Branding Your PoD Business

Every business has a personality. The problem is that many businesses acquire their personalities by chance. Unfortunately, many such businesses rarely thrive. All they achieve is survival. That's not how you should approach the building of your PoD business. Everything you do to build it should be thought out carefully and be designed to achieve a specific objective. Everything done in your business either builds its personality or destroys it.

To ensure you build a business that your customers love and enjoy running, you need to go through the personality-building process. Before looking at how to do this, let's first understand the concepts of *brand* and *branding*.

Brand, Branding, and Brand Identity Defined

Can you believe that you have already begun building a PoD brand? The work you've done contributes significantly to brand building, as shown shortly. Let's first clarify what a brand, branding, and brand identity mean. In the process, you'll also discover how these three concepts differ.

What Is a Brand?

What comes to mind when you hear or see the name Walmart? Perhaps you start thinking about low-cost products or any number of things known about the company. Whatever it is that you associate Walmart with, you've just had a taste of the power of a brand. The perception you have about Walmart is certainly different from how you perceive Target, one of its competitors.

A brand is all that customers observe about a company and includes their experiences, what they see and hear, as well as how they feel about its products or services. For many people, a brand is the logo and name of a company. Although these two elements are part of a brand, they're not the brand itself. A brand encompasses both the seen and unseen, including how the public feels about it.

A brand, especially when carefully thought out and designed, differentiates a business from another. This means your brand can make you the preferred company for a select group of customers. If your brand is associated with better-than-average customer service, you can be sure of continued customer loyalty. Because of its power, brands are often protected with trademarks and other similar legal protection tools.

What Branding Means

The process that strategically builds a brand is called branding. All the activities such as building your business' website, promoting your business, or designing an image for your PoD products belong to branding. One of the easiest ways of thinking about branding is as the method of making your brand visible.

There are three powerful reasons for branding.

1. **It's a way to differentiate your business.** PoD products like white T-shirts are all the same before printing them. If your business and your competitors sold them as they are, yours won't be different from those of your rivals. Brand your T-shirts and, immediately, your products will be different from your competitors'.

2. **It makes your business easily recognizable.** If you visited Best Buy and Amazon's websites, how would you tell that you're on one and not the other? Of course, you'll look at things like logos and copy. That should convince you immediately that branding will make it easy to recognize your business. It's for this reason that branding gets applied in all communication materials whether brochures, flyers, advertisements, blogs, or packaging.

3. **Branding helps keep customers.** Customers want to know what to expect when they do business with you. Because branding is by design consistent, it makes customers feel a

certain way. It's this experience that keeps them buying from you, which helps maintain a loyal customer base.

What Is Brand Identity?

How do you often differentiate one brand from the other? The simplest brand tool millions of people use is the logo. Yes, the logo is one of the elements that help identify a brand. It's easy to identify these other elements when you think of brand identity as a visual and communication representation of a particular brand.

Have you figured out what other elements make a brand recognizable? You probably mentioned things such as brand name, products, taglines, packaging, and signature customer service.

The central part of brand identity is design. This includes bringing together the tagline, logo, brand name, color palette, graphic elements, typography, and brand voice or tone. The outcome of brand design is a brand image or identity.

These three elements—brand, branding, and brand identity—work together to create a cohesive and consistent image of a brand in the mind of the customer. By developing a strong brand and brand identity, your business can build customer loyalty, create a strong reputation, and differentiate itself in your niche and industry.

Guide to Creating Your Brand

How do you create a brand that your buyer persona loves? You create a brand that has the characteristics and values that they like. That's why you had to go over the steps to define your niche. The process culminated with defining your value proposition. This alone isn't enough to complete the creation of a brand.

You still need to answer why your business exists. Yes, you want to make money but that's the same for every other business; you can't differentiate your business this way. You need to define the purpose of your business, which should align with your buyer persona.

Fortunately, you would have discovered why your ideal customer buys certain products or services. Write a single statement that clearly specifies what your company stands for and what values it espouses.

When you've finished defining your business' purpose, it's time to create brand assets: visual elements, messaging, and experiences. Let's go over how to do this.

Visual Elements

The quickest way to differentiate your business from competitors is by using visual elements such as the logo, color palette, typography, graphic elements, and imagery. The most important of these are the logo, color palette, and typography.

- **Logo:** The logo is the most prominent visual element that most people see first. It must resonate with your buyer persona and communicate what your business stands for. You can head over to Thesaurus.com to find synonyms that describe your company's reason for existence. Then, find a free online logo maker and try different designs. Make sure that you read the next two bullet points before designing your logo.

- **Color palette:** Color is powerful because it's associated with certain emotions. That's why there's psychology dedicated to color and emotions. Consider this: 57% and 35% of men and women, respectively, prefer the blue color. If your buyer persona is male, don't you think including blue in visual elements would be a good decision? The colors you choose should align with the brand personality you want to convey. For instance, if you want to showcase power, include green, while blue means tranquility.

- **Typography:** This deals with the type of fonts you use on your test. While the fonts are key, you also need to consider their size, color, contrast, and shape. Your typography should be unique and resonate with your logo. When choosing a font family, at most three types, consider the emotions you want to elicit. Ask yourself what your font hierarchy says about your business' priorities.

Messaging

Do you remember the value proposition you defined when choosing your niche? Great. It's now time to communicate it to your ideal target buyer. Brand messaging is the way you communicate your value proposition to entice your buyer persona to buy repeatedly from you. Additionally, you need to include your values in your messaging.

The way you communicate your messaging counts. This means that you need to choose a voice and tone that resonate with your ideal buyer. You can find the tone that aligns with your ideal buyer in your market research. Coupled with this, figure out what descriptive words define your brand. For instance, your brand voice might showcase confidence, authority, or fun.

The values you espouse and your brand voice guide you on what you say and how you say it. Again, your brand voice comes from why your company exists.

Sometimes it takes a few iterations before you come up with the right brand messaging. Let this process unfold, and you'll soon land on the kind of messaging your ideal customer loves.

Customer Experiences

You have two choices when it comes to customer experience (CX) when they interact with your business: You can let it happen by chance, or you can intentionally design it. Creating it is the best bet because you can align it with all the elements of your brand.

When your customer interacts with your brand, they go away with certain perceptions called CX. For instance, they may think that your customer service will do with improvement. It's not hard to figure out if your customers have had wonderful experiences or not. When they stop buying from your business, you know that they're not happy with something.

Fortunately, you can define ahead of time what kind of customer service and quality you want your customers to have. Ask yourself what you would want your customers to say to their friends, colleagues, and families. Hopefully, you want them to say what your brand stands for in everything it does.

Now, complete the following checklist to ensure that you apply what you've learned in this chapter before tackling the next one.

Checklist

	Write down all your passions or interests in preparation for identifying your PoD business niche. Research the market and study the competition for each passion or interest to define your niche.
	Define your buyer persona and be as specific as possible, study the competition vying for your buyer persona, and define your value proposition.
	Define the purpose of your business. Note that this isn't "to make profit." Instead, answer why your business exists.
	Decide what visual elements—logo, fonts, colors—you're going to use for your brand.
	Figure out the messaging of your brand to ensure it resonates with your ideal buyers.
	Define the kind of customer experience your brand aims to deliver

Chapter 3:

How to Source In-Demand Quality

Products

While finding a business niche is crucial, it doesn't tell you what PoD products to sell. Knowing the kind of product to sell requires different knowledge and skills. When you've identified the product to sell, you need to locate a reliable white-label product supplier. This chapter focuses on helping you find the right PoD product and supplier.

What Kind of Product Are You Going to Sell?

The kinds of PoD products you can sell are limitless. You can sell items such as T-shirts, hoodies, mugs, pillowcases, bags, watches, and wall art. Deciding which of these products to sell can be a daunting task, but one you must do to have a PoD business. If you keep in mind that your business serves the needs and wants of your buyer persona, you'll find the right product to sell. Here are some ideas that will help you identify your PoD product:

Browse Online Marketplaces

Marketplaces such as Etsy, eBay, and Amazon are great for identifying products you could sell. To illustrate, let's use the Amazon Best Sellers list to decide on what product to sell.

Head over to amazon.com/best-sellers/zgbs to access the Amazon Best Sellers list. Your screen will be filled with best-selling products from the categories listed on the left pane. Clicking on one of these categories returns a list of the 100 best-selling products in that category or department as Amazon calls it. For instance, clicking on the clothing category brings up a list of 100 products, including shoes, T-shirts, belt bags, tank tops, socks, and shorts.

You can search further according to the subcategories given on the left pane. For example, in the clothing category, you can search which products make the list of the best-selling clothing for men, girls, women, or boys.

What's exciting about clothing is that you can find out what material was used to manufacture them. This information can come in handy when you discuss your requirements with the white-label product supplier.

If you don't get ideas from Amazon, you can go to Etsy and check for products trending currently. All it takes is visiting Etsy.com and searching for "trending now." Etsy brings up a huge list of products for inspiration. Go over the list and note down ideas that come to mind as you do so. As you do this, keep your ideal buyer in mind. You might get design ideas to use on your products.

It's advisable to keep an open mind when looking for product ideas on marketplaces. The reason is that these sources have all kinds of products, some of which you may never have thought about.

When looking for a product, you need to decide whether you want one that sells throughout the year or during certain seasons. Even if a product sells during some seasons, you can consider it. However, you'll need to find others that sell during different seasons so that your business makes money throughout the year.

Ideally, consider choosing a product that sells throughout the year. This helps a great deal when automating your business or when you want predictable revenue. You can check on Google Trends to find out how consistently people search for keywords related to your product.

If you can, stay away from trending products at the start of your business. The risk of trending products is that sales can stop abruptly, which will negatively impact your revenues.

Consider the Product Idea You Have

While you were figuring out what business niche to go in, you may have conceived various product ideas. Some of the popular products that sell well in the PoD industry include T-shirts, hoodies, hats, caps, and phone accessories. Whatever product idea you may have, it's worth checking if it's selling on marketplaces such as the ones mentioned above.

When you've found the kind of product to sell, you need to find its white-label supplier. There's a possibility that you could find a product and fail to find a PoD manufacturer who supplies it.

Product Sourcing and Its Importance

With a niche and product identified, your next step is to source the product. It's vital to know how best to source the product and what to look for when sourcing it. In this section, you'll learn what product sourcing is, how to do it effectively, and its importance.

Product Sourcing Defined

Product sourcing means searching and finding a product to sell from a supplier. You can source products from wholesale suppliers or makers of white-label products. For a PoD business, you ideally should source your products from manufacturers of white-label products. If you sell a large volume of white-label products, partnering with a dropshipper might be your best bet.

Product sourcing is the process of buying product inventory from a supplier and then reselling it to your target customer. You can source products in a variety of ways, including forming a partnership with a dropshipper, buying from a personalized products' maker, and purchasing third-party goods from a wholesale supplier.

The Importance of Product Sourcing

Product sourcing is a crucial part of your supply chain—the process from raw materials to fulfillment of orders. A slight problem in product sourcing will delay the fulfillment of orders, which in turn, will drag down your revenues. This alone tells you how important product sourcing is. Other benefits of effective product sourcing include the following:

- **Ensures your product meets your customer requirements**. The final product you sell is as good as the raw materials that make it. Product sourcing helps make sure that the right materials are used in the making of your product. This results in producing quality products that your customers are happy with. To appreciate the power of sourcing, imagine that you happen to sell poor-quality products.

  What do you think will happen to your business? Its reputation and revenue will drop because customers will bad-mouth your business. The number of bad reviews will escalate, which will repel people from buying from you. It goes without saying that it serves you well to product-source effectively.

- **Facilitates faster fulfillment times**. The advancement of technology has made many shoppers impatient. We live in instant gratification times. Once a customer orders a product, they expect fast delivery. Poor product sourcing strategies will fail to support this customer expectation. As you can guess, your business will suffer. Contrarily, well-run product sourcing helps you keep your order fulfillment promises, which is good for your business.

- **Helps resolve order fulfillment issues faster**. No one can guarantee that you'll always deliver products timely. Problems in the supply chain may occur. For instance, your supplier's production may break down, or they may struggle to source the raw materials needed. Product sourcing, when done properly, will ensure that there are backups to help address supply chain problems such as these.

The survival of your PoD business depends a lot on effective product sourcing. Not only will this ensure that products reach customers timely, but will also help build your business' reputation. This will, in turn, attract more sales and opportunities you may never have thought about such collaboration with larger online businesses.

Factors to Consider When Sourcing Products

When you identified the product to sell, it's not only its look that you considered; you also checked the kind of raw materials that were used to manufacture it. If you want to sell clothing, you're fortunate because marketplaces like Amazon provide their composition. Right off the bat, you won't have to struggle to figure out what raw materials are needed and in what proportions. Some other products may require further research to identify their raw materials.

Other factors that you need to pay attention to include the following:

- **Product profitability.** Sourcing an expensive product is commendable if it delivers unparalleled quality. However, you may be forced to sell it at a higher price to make the desired profit margin. Your decision on the product will depend on the prices that your ideal buyer prefers, as well as your profit margin. It's a balancing act you should be prepared to make to sell good products that customers love while earning the desired profit.

- **Product value to your ideal buyer.** You should understand your ideal buyer better than anyone. This means that the product you choose must be a fit with this buyer to stand a chance of making target revenue.

- **Weight of the product.** One of the important costs for a PoD business is shipping expenses. Unless shipping is a flat rate, you or your customers will pay more for a heavy product than a lighter one. It's preferable to source lighter products to minimize the cost of shipping. Not only can this lower your business' operating costs, but may also encourage customers to buy if they pay for shipping.

Other factors we've already covered when learning to find products that sell and include your target buyer, and whether the product is a fad or evergreen. Once you know what product to source and factors to consider, it's time for the next step.

Find the Right Product Supplier

Once you've identified the main factors that will influence your buying decisions, it's time to find a manufacturer or supplier who fits the bill of the product you're looking for. Ideally, you want to source your products from a manufacturer because suppliers tend to be middlemen. As such, you could buy products more expensively than if you bought directly from the manufacturer.

A manufacturer sources the raw materials and produces your product from them. They may sell these products directly to consumers, but often they sell to retailers, wholesalers, or distributors. In the PoD industry, manufacturers produce white-label products. These are the products you need on which to print your design to fulfill customer orders.

A manufacturer of your white-label products is crucial for the success of your business. If you don't have these products, you can't sell to your customers, meaning that you have no business. That's why you need to thoroughly research potential manufacturers with an eagle eye. Most importantly, you'll need to have multiple manufacturers build the redundancy necessary to address issues when they arise.

At the end of the day, it's up to you whether to partner with a supplier or manufacturer. Keep in mind that going with a supplier often reduces your profit margins.

Looking for a manufacturer or supplier entails the following steps:

- **Step 1—Determine product requirements:** Earlier, you learned about how to find a product to sell. At this point, you should be clear about what raw materials are needed to manufacture your product. There should also be no doubt about the quality of the product you want. Additionally, you need to think about the price you're willing to pay for your white-label product. Figuring this out requires that you determine the gross profit margin you want and what percentage of cost is your product. Also, decide the time frames to have the product delivered for order fulfillment.

- **Step 2—Search for potential manufacturers:** The quickest method for finding potential manufacturers of your white-label products is checking on PoD marketplaces and platforms such as Printful, Printify, and Redbubble. Some of these online places allow you to search for manufacturers and suppliers. When you find a manufacturer you can use, add it to a list you'll evaluate later. If you don't mind having foreign manufacturers, consider searching on Google, Bing, and Alibaba.

- **Step 3—Evaluate potential manufacturers:** Go over each of the potential manufacturers on the list created above. Check them against your product requirements, study their customer reviews, and if possible, also assess their prices and delivery timeframes. Based on your findings, create a shortlist of possible manufacturers you could use. Have at least five manufacturers on your final list.

- **Step 4—Request quotes:** Ask for quotes from each of the manufacturers on the list created above. Make sure you ask if they have minimum order quantities (MOQs) and offer custom orders. Ensure that each manufacturer itemizes all the costs involved to deliver the product to your desired destination. Some manufacturers offer exclusivity, which is great for a PoD business. As mentioned above, also ask the potential manufacturer to send their terms and conditions in detail.

- **Step 5—Choose your final manufacturer or two:** A good way to evaluate the quotes you received is to organize the data in a spreadsheet. One of the columns should have what you require from a manufacturer per time such as pricing, delivery timeframes, quality, and quantity. Out of this analysis, choose one or two manufacturers that align with your needs.

- **Step 6—Negotiate terms:** When it comes to business dealings, resolve to negotiate everything. You can negotiate things such as payment terms, MOQs, and delivery timeframes. MOQs can make it difficult if you don't have the funds to pay for large product quantities. This makes it even more important to negotiate MOQs. Understand that it may be tougher for the manufacturer to grant favorable payment terms at the start of the relationship with them. Still, it's worth a try, and perhaps offer to pay 80% of the agreed price. Whatever agreement you have with your manufacturer, make sure that it's covered in a written contract.

- **Step 7—Ask for samples:** Beginner PoD business owners often make the mistake of assuming that their manufacturer will deliver quality products. They get shocked when their first few customers complain about the quality of the products they received. The solution is to ask for or order samples before finalizing your decision on the manufacturer to buy from. When happy with the quality, you can enter into a written contract with the chosen manufacturers.

- **Step 8—Manage manufacturer relationships:** Finding the kind of manufacturer who fits your requirements is only the beginning. The next thing to do is ensure that they keep delivering according to the agreement. This requires constantly reviewing their performance against expectations. When you feel things could improve, you give them feedback. You also need to maintain your end of the stick. If the manufacturer raises concerns, swiftly address them. Maintaining a working relationship with your manufacturer will come in handy when you expand your business.

While it's great having a manufacturer that meets all your requirements, it's possible for things to sour later. For this reason, be on the lookout for potential manufacturers you could work with. This doesn't weaken your business but strengthens it.

Why and How to Outsource PoD Order Fulfillment

The aim of business is to make a profit, but its purpose is to make life meaningful for its customers. By making customers happy after they've placed orders, a business makes a profit. Loyal customers are even better because they can buy over and over, increasing the value of the business. Order fulfillment is an important instrument for exciting your PoD customers.

Order fulfillment includes everything that happens once a customer has placed an order to when they receive their product. For PoD business, this involves producing, packing, and delivering the product timely. Poor order fulfillment can drag your business' reputation into the mud, no matter how great your product marketing and sales are.

Luckily, as a beginner, you can have an effective order fulfillment process by outsourcing it to third parties. Because order fulfillment can be time-consuming and resource-intensive, your business can benefit in many ways by outsourcing.

The Case for Outsourcing PoD Order Fulfillment

Order fulfillment outsourcing involves partnering with a third-party company. This company uses its resources to fulfill orders on your behalf. As a result, you or your business can benefit in numerous ways, including these:

1. **Allows you to sell to a wider audience.** Surprising as it may sound, your buyer persona doesn't stay in one country, state, or continent. You could find them both locally, nationally, and internationally. Imagine how hard it would be to deliver a product to a customer in Australia while you're in the US! You'd need to figure out shipping rates and a whole other set of factors.

    To avoid doing this, you'd simply sell to customers locally, and perhaps nationally. This limits the revenue you can make. Outsourcing allows you to reach many more customers and still deliver an excellent CX. This is because order fulfillment companies have the expertise and network to allow you to sell to anyone anywhere.

2. **Decreases shipping costs.** It's understandable that outsourcing order fulfillment costs money. Think about it, what business activity doesn't cost money? The important thing is not the cost, but the ROI you gain for the cost you spend. Effective order fulfillment excites customers and can turn them into loyal ones. This will result in increased revenue per customer. Moreover, order fulfillment companies typically have facilities across various locations. This allows them to ship products cheaper to a variety of customers. This, in turn, increases your profit margin.

3. **Allows you to provide accurate delivery information to your customers.** Online buyers want to know when they're likely to receive their product before they buy. If your online store doesn't provide shipping times, you'll likely lose many customers. Also, long delivery times may repel customers from buying because we live in a world where everything needs to occur fast.

    Third-party fulfillment companies have the manpower, resources, and experience to handle shipping challenges. As such, you can confidently display estimated shipping times of products on your online store. They know how to handle shipping difficulties and still provide great customer service. This will encourage more customers to buy, especially if you offer shorter delivery times.

4. **It ships products faster.** Third-party order fulfillment companies tend to have multiple facilities. Outsourcing order fulfillment places your products closer to your customers. As a result, customers receive their products faster, which is good for the reputation of your business.

Order fulfillment can turn out to be your competitive edge if you outsource it. Of course, it's not necessary to outsource for the sake of it. Your business will dictate whether outsourcing fulfillment is the right thing or not. By definition, a PoD business outsources order fulfillment. It's still important to understand the reasons that could cause a PoD business to outsource order fulfillment. Here are some of the drivers for outsourcing this function:

- **You don't have the expertise to do it yourself.** Although a PoD business generally outsources order fulfillment, you're not obliged to. If you have the order fulfillment expertise and resources, you can do this function yourself. Otherwise, it's a better move to outsource order fulfillment because the learning curve can be steep, and you'll need to invest a lot of money upfront. As mentioned earlier, outsourcing allows you to benefit from someone's expertise and resources.

- **Your business expands to new locations.** Expanding an online business is easy because you don't need to invest in physical locations. For a PoD business, this brings the challenge of getting products to customers on time. The way to surmount this obstacle is by outsourcing order fulfillment. You can find order fulfillment companies closer to the locations where you have customers. Alternatively, you can partner with an order fulfillment company that has numerous facilities across a wider geographic area.

- **If fast shipping is your priority.** To be competitive, you have no choice but to deliver customer products quickly. You can't afford to deliver products to customers later than most of your competitors do. Otherwise, you'll lose customers and put your business in danger of bankruptcy. For fast shipping, an order fulfillment company is your best bet.

- **You have too many shipments to make.** You might have the order fulfillment expertise and handle it yourself. However, your marketing and sales may bring in too many customers, making it hard to keep up with shipments. Your best bet is to outsource some or all of your order fulfillment functions.

- **Your order fulfillment expenses are too high.** Whether you're handling order fulfillment yourself or outsourcing it, you incur some costs. Your order fulfillment expenses may be too high relative to outsourcing this function. If having higher profit margins appeals to you—and it should—outsourcing order fulfillment is the way to go.

By now, you should be clear on what the way forward is regarding outsourcing order fulfillment. With the benefits that it confers, it's a good idea to consider outsourcing it.

Factors to Consider When Choosing an Order Fulfillment Company

Now that you've decided to outsource your order fulfillment function, it's time to learn about finding the right partner. At a minimum, the order fulfillment you choose should do a better job than you could. You don't only outsource to a company but to a partner. This suggests that you and your partner should act in the best interest of both parties.

The following factors help with making sure that you choose the right order fulfillment partner.

Supplier Reviews and Net Promoter Score

Just as consumers can review brands, so can businesses review order fulfillment companies they hire. Before outsourcing your order fulfillment, check those reviews to ensure that you make an informed decision.

For effective evaluation of an order fulfillment company, read both positive and negative reviews. Any potential order fulfillment company should consistently receive glowing reviews about shipping times, communication, inventory management, and customer service. If you find a company that doesn't do too well in these, avoid it. You don't want to sit with order fulfillment troubles you could have prevented.

While reviews are helpful, you can go a step further and check the order fulfillment company's net promoter score (NPS). This metric tells you how positively customers consider the services of a company. An order fulfillment company with a higher NPS suggests that its customers are loyal to it, while a lower one means the opposite. Furthermore, a higher NPS means that more customers believe that they can recommend the company, which is great.

Order Fulfillment Costs

As you know, there's a cost associated with order fulfillment. The lower this cost is for a given quality of service, the better it is for your profits. You should know each of the expenses that make up the total order fulfillment costs. This helps avoid any misunderstanding when you have to pay your order fulfillment partner.

The main order fulfillment expenses to know include the following:

- **Order preparation costs:** When your customer places an order, the fulfillment company picks and packs the product. They then label the package and ready it for shipping. Since doing this requires resources, it costs money to select and package a customer's order. Request your order fulfillment company to specify what this cost is.

- **Warehouse storage fee:** Your PoD might not keep inventory, but your order fulfillment company has to store a certain number of white-label products in their inventory. You'd need to agree with your order fulfillment partner on what level of stock to keep, especially if your white-label products are unique. If you print your design on generic white-label products, you might not have to worry too much about what level of inventory needs to be maintained. Even then, your order fulfillment partner may charge a certain fee to keep stock of your desired white-label products. Get your partner to specify how much this fee is.

- **Shipping costs:** Typically, order fulfillment companies work with certain carriers. Order fulfillment companies are seen as important allies by their shipping partners. This gives the order fulfillment companies some room to negotiate shipping rates. As such, working with a given order fulfillment company may provide access to lower shipping rates.

- **Miscellaneous order fulfillment fees:** Some order fulfillment companies may charge various kinds of fees. For example, they may charge you a kitting, receiving inventory, returns processing, or long-term storage fee. A kitting fee is the cost of catering to the needs of your PoD business in the order management system. Unpacking and storing products costs money, which can be a part of an expense called a receiving inventory fee.

A returns processing fee may be charged when your customer returns your product. If your white-label products aren't being converted into a final product, you might be charged a long-term storage fee. Make sure you know all the kinds of extra fees that every order fulfillment company you're considering charges for easy comparison with its peers.

Communication

Any partnership thrives where there's transparent communication. A lot can go wrong in order fulfillment. For instance, there may be issues that prevent the timely shipping of your customers' orders. It's essential that you know about such issues on time, including what possible solutions are. This will simplify decision-making and communication with your customers.

To figure out if a potential fulfillment company communicates transparently, check their reviews, testimonials, and social media pages. Be careful of testimonials, as they can be filtered before being shared publicly. Rely more on customer reviews.

Ecommerce Integration

A PoD business' online store needs to be automatically linked to an order fulfillment company. As such, every potential order fulfillment partner you're considering should integrate with your online store platform. As mentioned earlier, this will allow your customer information to immediately filter to the order fulfillment company for faster delivery.

Location

In the beginning, when you're still gaining experience, it's worthwhile considering an order fulfillment company that's closer to where you stay. This will allow you to visit their operations and learn how things work within an order fulfillment company. As your business grows, you'll be able to outsource order fulfillment much more effectively.

Look for experienced order fulfillment companies that have multiple facilities across locations where your buyers are. This helps speed up shipping and lower delivery costs.

Many order fulfillment companies tend to harp too much about the volume of orders they've fulfilled without saying anything about product quality. As you evaluate a potential order fulfillment partner, consider if they have demonstrated the ability to supply the right product quality and quantity. When you assess an order fulfillment company, request they furnish you with their product record in the past year to 3 years. This should be compared with the volume that was required.

A good order fulfillment company will have records of the quality of products they produce. You can ask to see those records that cover the past 12 months. Also, consider how they ensure they produce quality products almost all the time. Find out what happens when they produce a product that the customer returns due to quality reasons. It's crucial to be clear which party is responsible for correcting the problem. Yes, the customer is yours, and you should lead the effort to correct the problem. However, you shouldn't be responsible when it comes to the cost of fixing the issue.

Lead Time

When your customer places an order, your fulfillment company produces the product, packs, labels it, and ships it. All these activities take time. How fast these tasks are completed may vary from one company to the next. That's why you need to know how long it takes your potential order fulfillment company to complete this series of tasks.

You'll need to tell your customers how long it takes before they receive their order at the checkout. You'll be guided by your order fulfillment partner's lead time when making this promise.

Payment Terms

In the PoD industry, you're usually charged for the product, its production, and shipping as soon as your customer places an order.

There's no law that says you should pay immediately. You can negotiate with your order fulfillment company to pay for the previous month's order the following month.

The reason this might be a good option is that some of your customers may return orders they're unhappy with. How you deal with this will depend on the negotiation between you and your order fulfillment partner. Paying later provides both of you with the time to reconcile issues before making the payment.

If you can arrange payment terms, you can better handle financial challenges when they surface.

Customer Support Availability

Just as your customers will want a swift customer service response, so should you expect a similar service from your fulfillment partner. When things don't turn out as well as desired, you will need to contact your order fulfillment company. You can imagine how frustrating it would be if it takes 24 hr before getting a response!

Ideally, choose a fulfillment company that provides 24/7 support. Check how efficient this customer support is by reading customer reviews.

Once all of this is in place, the next thing would be setting up monitoring and communication systems to ensure everything moves smoothly. We'll talk more about the order fulfillment process in Chapter 5.

Complete the checklist below to ensure that you have a product and its manufacturer to prepare for the next chapter.

Checklist

	Decide on the product that you're going to launch your PoD

	business with. Remember that you're chosen product should be in demand, preferably throughout the year.
	Search and find a product manufacturer that meets all your requirements such as the kind of product, quality, and pricing.
	Look for an order fulfillment company with proven capacity to deliver to PoD customers

Chapter 4:

Marketing and Sales

All the work you've done above has prepared you to start making sales. But before you make sales, you need to get your marketing strategy and marketing plans into place. Fortunately, you've already done some of the hard work, such as analyzing your competition and defining your buyer persona.

In this chapter, you'll learn about the customer journey, why you need to understand it, marketing strategy, and how to create a marketing plan. Let's dive in right away.

Customer Journey and Why It's Important

Imagine Joy needs a new unique T-shirt branded with the image of a Samoyed. She searches online and finds one that sends her to your PoD business' website. She reads the product description and also checks other T-shirts. Instead of buying immediately, she researches other brands offering similar merchandise. A few days later, she gets a Facebook ad from one of the brands she looked at offering a discount for the T-shirt she wants. She buys the T-shirt because she likes the idea of saving money.

The following day, she receives her T-shirt, wears it, takes a selfie, and posts it on social media. Because of the CX she enjoyed, Joy recommends the brand that sold her the T-shirt. A month later, she buys a similar T-shirt for her son, who likes Samoyeds too.

Does the above story sound familiar? If you do online shopping, you probably went through a similar experience. The process or the path that Joy went through is called the customer journey. Most customers, online or offline, usually follow that kind of path to buy something. Think of the customer journey as the process a customer goes through from learning about a brand until they buy and what happens after that.

Every PoD business owner needs to understand the customer journey to optimize their customers' experiences. That way, the business can get its customers to buy often, which is great for generating profits. Additionally, understanding your customer's journey allows you to use the right kind of marketing. Otherwise, you'll waste a lot of money because of marketing wrongly.

The customer journey consists of five stages, as discussed below.

Stage 1: Awareness

At this stage, the prospect is aware that they have a problem or want a certain product. They start searching for the solution or the product. Your business should make a good first impression to excite the prospect into considering what they offer. For instance, your brand should stand out while your online store should be easy to use.

One of the powerful ways of making a powerful first impression is to provide education. For example, if you sell T-shirts, you could have content that helps the customer make an informed buying decision, such as a blog post titled, "What to Look for When Buying T-Shirts Online." If you're running advertisements to these people, you could have such content as an ebook.

Failure to approach potential customers who're at this stage means you can't make sales from them. As you'll see when we discuss the marketing channel, this stage has the largest number of people who could become your customers. If you do a good job here, you could end up making a ton of sales.

Stage 2: Consideration

In the second stage, a prospective customer evaluates options. For a customer looking to buy a backpack, consideration might look like the following.

The potential customer has combed through numerous options and narrowed down their options to two companies: The Bag Company and Top Merchandise. They now conduct further research, comparing prices, features, and customer reviews. When they check the prices, they find that both companies are affordable.

However, customer reviews tilt the scale in favor of The Bag Company because it provides excellent customer service and offers a one-year guarantee for its backpacks. The potential customer also finds that other past customers have had their backpacks replaced if they didn't meet the quality described.

Do you see why you needed to research and understand your competition? When it comes time for prospective customers to decide who to buy from, your positioning can win you sales—an enormous number of sales. This is where your value proposition will come in handy. You need to be unique to have an unfair advantage over the competition.

One of the ways you can be unique is by showing the pain you go through to source quality raw materials to produce your products. You can do this by creating a video showing this process.

How do you get customer reviews if you're just starting your business? Simply offer sample products in exchange for reviews.

Stage 3: Decision to Purchase

At this stage, the potential customers turn into buying customers. They have completed their research and decided on their best option. You need to make it easy for a person to purchase from your business.

Sometimes, some prospects may need a little push to make a purchase. You can offer discounts good for limited periods coupled with one or two customer reviews.

Stage 4: Customer Retention

We've mentioned earlier that it's vital to keep customers for as long as possible. Not only is it cheaper to get a customer to buy again, but your customer is likely to send new customers your way. For a customer to stay with you suggests that you must be doing something right as far as they're concerned. The big question is how do you retain a customer in a PoD business?

There are numerous methods of getting your customers to buy from you again, including the following:

- **Follow up after the purchase.** Interacting with your customers after they've purchased from you indicates that you care. People will buy again because they'll feel valued. Since few businesses make follow-ups after the sale, you'll likely stand out from your peers. There are many ways of making follow-ups, such as calling or emailing a customer and asking if they're happy with their purchase. The nice thing is that you can automate this in your PoD business. While doing this, you might spot opportunities to make upsells and thereby increase your revenues.

- **Employ surveys or other customer feedback.** It can be hard to know how people feel about their purchase experiences unless you ask them. A survey is a great way to find out how they felt while buying from you. The results from the surveys you run, when analyzed, will show you where you can improve user experience.

- **Send a company newsletter at regular intervals.** There's no better excuse for staying in touch with your customers than sending them your newsletter. Doing this differs markedly from sending promotional emails weekly or monthly. A newsletter has a higher perceived value and is cost-effective to send to your customers. You can also make offers in your newsletter. If it's a good newsletter, your customers won't wait to receive it. Some may share it with friends, colleagues, and family members, which can be a way to get new customers.

Always be on the lookout for best practices in customer retention. Most crucially, take one of those ideas and implement it immediately.

Stage 5: Loyalty or Advocacy

If you've done a great job from stage 1 to stage 4, your customer becomes loyal to your brand. Customer loyalty isn't something you get, but something you have to earn. You achieve this by offering the best value the customer has ever seen. This doesn't mean doing extraordinary things, but doing common things very well.

It's when customers buy from you often that they can become your advocate. This means that they turn into your salesperson, recommending your products to others.

Customers who interact and buy from your brand may be rewarded with loyalty programs. When done right, they can be a great way to not only retain customers but also attract new ones. You need to assess if your type of customer prefers loyalty programs or not. The reason is that most consumers prioritize value, convenience, and availability.

Understanding a Marketing Funnel

How you market to your potential customers can either give them positive or negative experiences. Ideally, you want to deliver great user experiences from the time a potential customer first interacts with your brand and beyond. It's for this reason that you need to understand the customer journey.

The way you guide your potential customer throughout their shopping experience is called customer flow. When you understand your customer journey, you can design every touchpoint so that you provide the best user experience possible. That's one of the reasons understanding a marketing funnel is necessary.

What comes to mind when you read or hear about the word "funnel"? For many, they conjure the image of a tool used to direct a liquid into a container with a narrow neck. This tool is wide at the top and progressively narrows down toward its bottom. Its end is a narrow tube for easy entering into a small opening.

The idea of a funnel entered into marketing folklore in 1898. It was inducted into the hall of marketing language by an advertising advocate known as E. St. Elmo Lewis. Because it simplifies marketing, a marketing funnel has become ubiquitous in the business world, especially online.

A marketing funnel is a tool that helps you visualize the steps a person follows from when they become aware of your brand until they become a customer. The simplest marketing funnel has four steps:

- **Step 1—Attention:** A potential customer becomes aware of your product or service through a social media post, colleague or friend, or advertisement. Another way a prospective customer can learn about your brand is through content marketing. They search for a term through a search engine such as Google or Bing and find brands such as yours. They then click on your website to learn more. This step corresponds with the first stage of the customer journey.

- **Step 2—Interest:** The prospective buyer immediately thinks that they need what you offer. They then start researching your product and may also consider competitor products.

- **Step 3—Desire:** The prospective customer wants to buy. So, they narrow down their options and choose one that best meets their needs. Steps 2 and 3 of the marketing funnel are intended to provide the prospective customer with enough information to make a decision.

- **Step 4—Action:** The prospect purchases and becomes a customer. This process is called a conversion. This step makes it for the prospective buyer to become a customer. For instance, you make sure that your checkout process works perfectly by testing it before you launch your PoD business.

Keep what you've learned in mind as you go through the creation of a marketing strategy and marketing plans.

Create Your Marketing Strategy

Understanding your competitors reveals how you can gain an upper hand over them. It also feeds into your marketing strategy; a strategy indicates what needs to be done to produce marketing that makes achieving your business goals possible. A well-crafted marketing strategy for a small business includes the following:

- marketing goals

- your buyer persona

- value proposition and messaging

- marketing budget

- marketing channels

- success metrics

- marketing plan

We have already looked at the main foundations of creating a marketing strategy: competitor analysis, messaging, value proposition, understanding your audience, defining your buyer persona, and understanding your niche. In this section, we'll guide you on how to define the remaining elements.

What Is a Marketing Strategy and What Is Its Benefit?

A marketing strategy is a high-level view that shows what you want to achieve and what marketing channels you're going to use to get there. Don't confuse a marketing strategy with a marketing plan. A marketing plan goes into the details of the things you're going to do and how you're going to do them to realize your marketing goals. That's why a marketing plan is an element of the marketing strategy for small businesses.

There are vital reasons you need a marketing strategy. The most important of these are as follows:

- **It aligns your brand messaging to ensure consistency.** When discussing brand messaging earlier, we emphasized the importance of being consistent in every channel you use. Because a marketing strategy includes brand messaging, it helps build and strengthen your brand's identity.

- **It helps you reach the right customers.** You can't craft a great marketing strategy without understanding who your ideal target audience is. That's why you had to research the market and analyze the competition before creating brand messaging. You want to make sure that your message aligns with your target audience. As such, a good marketing strategy will help you reach the right audience and increase your chances of making sales.

- **A marketing strategy guides your marketing efforts.** As a small business owner, you don't have a huge marketing budget. You can't absorb the marketing mistakes you make. For this reason, you need a marketing guide that ensures you market to the right people, reach out with the appropriate message, and use the right channels. Your marketing strategy will force you to align all these three key marketing components of effective marketing.

- **It helps you focus on the right marketing channels**. How many marketing channels are you aware of? Said another way, how many ways do companies market their products or services to you? If your experience is like ours, there are many, including social media, direct mail, TV, email, newspapers, magazines, and website ads. Which of these channels are you going to use in your business? Your marketing strategy will help you answer that question. Furthermore, you'll know where to direct your limited funds to get the best returns for your money as possible.

- **It helps you stay focused.** A marketing strategy requires you to set marketing goals linked to your business strategy. Goals give you something to channel your energy and efforts to. As a result, you can stay focused and avoid taking actions that don't help you achieve your business goals.

How to Create a Marketing Strategy

If realizing the above business benefits resonates with you, you can't wait to learn how to create an effective marketing strategy. We'll follow a step-by-step process to make doing this easy to follow and execute. Let's get started.

Step 1: Define Your Marketing End Goal

Why do you need to have an overarching marketing goal or objective? When you don't have a focal point, you try to focus everywhere. The problem is that you'll be left making no sense of anything. In marketing, if you don't have a goal to focus your ideas and efforts, you'll achieve minimally. You might even run a business that keeps hemorrhaging money left, right, and center, and not know what's wrong.

Co-Schedule, a company that helps marketers organize their activities, once conducted a survey among marketers. One of the questions it asked said, "Do you set marketing goals?" Unfortunately, 30% of marketers didn't set such goals. Interestingly, marketers who set goals are nearly four times more successful than those who don't.

For a business owner starting from scratch, your primary aim is to sell merchandise and make money. It follows that your business' primary aim should be to generate revenue at a profit. We're not saying building brand awareness isn't important, but it should come as a natural outcome of generating revenue. You don't have a huge marketing budget to primarily focus on brand awareness as giant corporations do. Knowing this, you can forge ahead and set your marketing goal.

Setting marketing goals can be frustrating if you don't know how. To set goals you can achieve, you should consider following the SMART goal-setting approach. SMART is an acronym for specific, measurable, attainable, relevant, and time-bound. Here's how this approach works:

- **Specific:** This means that your marketing should be clear; there should be no doubt about what it is you want to achieve. If you say, "Our goal is to be profitable," it's clear that you're interested in profits, not revenue, email list, or conversion from prospect to lead. Even a person who doesn't know your business can tell what it is you want to achieve. For a startup, a revenue goal might even be better than any other goal.

- **Measurable:** How do you know you've achieved your goal? You not only make it specific but also measurable. This means you have to have the numbers that tell you whether you've achieved your goal or not. Saying "Our goal is to be profitable" isn't enough because there are different levels of profitability. For instance, you may generate profits at 5%, 10%, 13%, 24%, or 60% of your revenues. Which of these would define your success? You can only know if you define that level right off the bat. For instance, you could refine your profitability goal to "Our goal is to generate profit at 30% of our revenue." Isn't it easier to know if you've done well or not?

- **Achievable:** Let's take the discussion of our marketing goal example further. Is a 30% profit margin achievable in your kind of business? To answer this question, it's a good idea to check if your competitors are achieving it or not. The reason is that you don't want to start too high and set yourself up for failure and be demoralized. In the PoD industry, a 30% profit margin is seen as on the high end. Targeting around 15%–20% may be the right thing to do for your goal to be achievable. In the end, the research you've done will guide you on whether your goal is achievable or not.

- **Relevant:** There's one way of ensuring that your goal is relevant: It should be linked to your business goals. Your goal should lead to the achievement of your business goals. That's why you should first figure out your business goals before you start setting marketing goals. If your aim is to be profitable, any goal that leads to revenue increase or decreasing of expenses will be relevant. To test if your goal is relevant, ask yourself, "How does this goal help us achieve our business goals?"

- **Time-bound:** Which is better, achieving a goal such as generating a 30% profit margin in the next year or in the following 2 years? To make a fair comparison, we need to compare these goals over the same time period. Doing so shows that a 30% profit margin over a year is better than a 30% profit margin over 2 years (or 15% over a year). If your goal is to achieve a 30% profit margin over a year, your actions will need to be a bit more aggressive than achieving the same target over 2 years. It follows that adding time to the achievement of your goal is necessary. At best, this will inject urgency into your business activities. With no due date added, you'll likely dilly-dally when you should get things done.

There's nothing wrong with having one major goal and a few minor ones. However, you should set minor goals that you'll achieve as a result of going after the big one. You don't want to set two or more major goals because you can easily fail to nail either of them.

You've already created your brand messaging, you know your buyer, and now you should connect the two. Unless you reach your ideal buyer with your message, you can't achieve your business and marketing goals.

You connect your ideal buyer with your messaging by using marketing channels. Typically, you find what channels to use during your market research. The most common channels for PoD are either online or offline and include the following:

- **Search engines:** One of the powerful methods of reaching your ideal buyer is through search engines. You can do this in two ways: search engine optimization (SEO) or search engine marketing (SEM). SEO seeks to optimize the position of your website toward the top of search engine results pages for free. In contrast, SEM achieves the same objective through paid advertising. Whichever search engine approach you use, your aim should be to attract your ideal buyer to your customer journey.

- **Social media:** This marketing channel allows you to reach your ideal buyer through social media platforms such as Twitter (aka X), Pinterest, Facebook, TikTok, YouTube, Snapchat, and Instagram. Consider this: A typical adult American spends 2 ¼ hr on social media and 70% of the people who enjoy a positive business experience refer your brand to others. They gossip, look for trending news, and share their social life. Having your brand on social media humanizes it, especially if you do what individuals do on these platforms. However, only do the things that you know from your research that they'll resonate with your ideal buyer.

- **Email:** This marketing channel can deliver amazing results if it's used properly. It can generate 4 times better ROI than any other digital marketing channel and people who buy through email spend 138% more than in other methods. The power of email is that it allows you to communicate directly with your ideal buyer.

- **Webinars:** This is one of the newest marketing channels. A webinar is simply an online sales presentation that adds value to your audience. You can think of them as marketing booklets popularly used by direct mail companies. The book provides content aimed at persuading the reader to buy a certain product. Webinars are amazing because you can record them and use them to promote your brand or products over and over again.

- **Person-to-person:** While online marketing channels form an important element of marketing, you can't completely ignore in-person marketing. This approach involves someone promoting a brand directly to others, whether an individual or a group. It's more effective when you talk to a group because it's human interaction. Some of the ways for in-person marketing include trade shows, physical product launches, and sales events.

- **Direct mail:** This marketing channel has been the workhorse behind the growth of some of the well-known U.S. businesses, such as Sears. One of the powers of direct mail is that you can laser-target your ideal audience.

- **Podcast:** In the old days, radio was a widely popular marketing channel. Businesses could, and still do, promote their products and services through it. The development of technology makes a similar avenue available for the small entrepreneur. With a microphone, the right software, and a computer, you can start your podcast (which works like radio). Not only can you provide valuable content to your audience on it, but you can also promote your brand and products on it.

With so many marketing channels, which one should you choose in the beginning? The answer to this question depends on your goals and resources, such as your marketing budget. If you can pay for advertising, you can use SEM and social media because you can quickly generate leads.

Typically, it's worth choosing three channels that you know your audience uses. The reason we suggest using three is that these platforms can change how they work, and you could be left in the lurch if you use only one. A case in point is what happened years ago on Facebook. Back then, you could create a Facebook page for your business, post valuable content, and generate leads.

Facebook changed its algorithm to push businesses to reach their target audience through paid advertising. All businesses that relied on free Facebook promotions were left in distress. That's why we suggest using multiple channels.

Choose Format of Content

Gone are the days when people would buy from you simply because you had a good product or service. Even if people buy, you need ways to keep them coming back. There's nothing as effective at helping you do this as adding value to your customers through helpful information. That's why content marketing is a big part of most successful online businesses.

When you researched your market, you would have identified the kind of information your ideal buyer likes to consume. Additionally, it's vital to figure out what kind of format your ideal buyer prefers. Well-crafted and liked content can be a great tool to attract new customers as well. It makes sense to take advantage of this because you can find new customers with your content long after you've created it. Here are the popular types of content to consider:

- **Video:** Is it an accident that YouTube has become an important tool for searching for information online? What do YouTube and TikTok have in common? YouTube has become popular because it's a video platform and millions of people prefer this form of content. TikTok and YouTube both support the use of videos only to share content. The growth of these platforms suggest the likability of video by many of their users. It shouldn't come as a surprise that 92% of marketers generate positive ROI from their videos. This is important for a startup because you don't want to lose money due to a limited marketing budget.

- **Text-based content:** How many people read blog posts? It's an astonishing 77% of internet users. Since there are about five billion internet users globally, the number of blog readers is about 3.85 billion. It's clear that written content is popular across the world. You can also conclude that buyers in different types of niches read the written word. Combining video and the written word can be a great method of appealing to your ideal buyer. The good news is that you can create written content in many formats, including blog articles, white papers, transcripts of videos and audio, and ebooks.

- **Audio:** Before Earl Nightingale narrated his widely successful *"The Strangest Secret,"* audio was generally popular on radio and music. Since then, many publishers have created audiobooks and podcasts to tap into the audio-listening market. The highest percentage of Americans aged 12 and higher between 2020 and 2022 was 41%. In 2021, about 177 million Americans listened to a podcast. This points to the interest of Americans in listening to audio such as podcasts or audio recordings. Most importantly, this is an opportunity for you to reach your ideal buyer.

Video, written content, and audio are three powerful formats that are likely to resonate with your ideal buyer. However, you may have found in your market research that your buyer persona prefers video over the other two content formats. In that case, focus mostly on video content production. The same thing applies if they prefer written content or audio.

Step 3: Allocate a Marketing Budget

The purpose of marketing your brand or products is to make selling super simpler. It's possible to market your products for free, but that process can be slow. It requires you to use content to attract your ideal buyer. There's nothing wrong with this, but content marketing works great as a long-term customer-attraction method. You can consider combining it with other methods if you want your business to get going faster.

Whether you use content or you advertise your products, you still need a marketing budget. The reason is that there are numerous types of costs associated with marketing, including building a website, logo design, advertising, and content production. Your marketing budget should cover a certain period of time, such as a year. In this case, you want your marketing budget to help you achieve the goal you set above. If you want to achieve the goal within a year, your market budget should cover that period.

You already know your target audience, which marketing channels you're going to use, and the content format you'll employ. It's now time to estimate how much you'll spend to attract your target audience.

New businesses can plan to spend between 12% and 20% of their revenue on marketing. Let's imagine that you plan to sell 2,000 T-shirts at $25 per item in 2023. This means that your annual revenue in 2023 would be $50,000 (2,000 x $25 = $50,000). If you're going to use 16% of that revenue on marketing, then your marketing budget will be $8,000 in 2023.

This budget is high-level. You still need to have a budget based on your marketing plan. The maximum amount you can spend can't exceed $8,000 per year.

Step 4: Develop a Detailed Marketing Plan

A marketing plan is a marketing action plan. It shows the activities you're going to perform to contribute toward reaching the goal defined in your marketing strategy. You can create a general marketing plan or one for each of your chosen marketing channels. It's far more effective to create a marketing plan for each marketing channel so that you can get as granular as you can about your activities.

We'll illustrate how to create a powerful marketing plan for social media. The reason for choosing this kind of plan is that social media is a great marketing channel for all sorts of audiences. A marketing plan that focuses on social media is called a social media marketing plan. In the beginning, it's a good idea to focus on one marketing channel. As your business grows, you can, and should, add other channels to minimize risk.

Social Media Marketing Plan

Think of a social media marketing plan as an organized set of activities you'll perform on social media to achieve certain goals. It's a subset of your marketing strategy, meaning that its goals must feed into the objectives of your marketing strategy. Here's how to go about creating a social media marketing plan:

Step A: Set Your Social Media Marketing Goals

No social media marketing plan, or any other plan, can be effective unless you define why you need it in the first place. You need to be clear about your intent so that the activities you do can be relevant.

Let's assume that your overall marketing goal is to generate $50,000 in revenue. Since you're starting from scratch, you have no existing customers and you're unknown. It follows that you'll need to go after brand awareness before you start generating sales leads.

So, your social media goals for your target year may be as follows:

1. Reach 25,000 people monthly beginning from the first month.

2. Generate 1,000 leads per month from the 2nd month. This goal is relevant if you combine social media with email. Social media becomes your source of leads, and email converts the leads into customers.

Remember to use the SMART approach when setting your social media marketing goals.

Step B: Decide Which Social Media Platforms You'll Use

How many social media platforms are there on the internet? It's estimated that social media platforms number about 128. Can you imagine yourself using all those platforms to achieve the goals you set in Step 1? You can if you hire numerous people to help you. However, you'll need to have a lot more money to pay them.

It's a lot easier to focus on one or two platforms at the start. As your business grows, you can add others to further scale your company. The big question becomes, "Which social media platform do I begin with?" There's no easy answer to that question. Fortunately, you have performed market research and understand your buyer persona.

You can also use research information such as that from Pew Research Center to figure out which platforms have your kind of buyer. Armed with this knowledge, you only need to find out which platform hosts your type of buyer in large numbers. Consider beginning with top social media platforms such as Twitter, Pinterest, TikTok, Facebook, Instagram, LinkedIn, and YouTube.

Step C: Complete Your Profiles on Your Chosen Platforms

Every social media platform requires businesses to create profiles before using them. This is a good chance to showcase your brand and its messaging. An effective social media profile should have a cover photo, profile photo, your business' bio, and other details such as website and physical addresses.

The key when creating social media platforms is to keep your voice and tone and be consistent across all the platforms you use. This means that your profile photo on Facebook should be similar to that on LinkedIn if you use those two platforms. This applies to all the other profile elements.

You don't have to be a graphic designer to create social media images. There are tools such as Canva and Pablo that have image templates for popular social media platforms.

When describing your PoD business, make sure that you clearly present your value proposition. People won't interact with your business unless they know what's in it for them. As a result, use as many keywords related to your PoD business as the given space allows. Don't forget to showcase the personality of your brand, mentioning why it exists or what it stands for.

Step D: Decide What Content to Post and When

You need to post content on your chosen social media platforms for your buyer to find you. It's right here when you need to decide what kind of content to post, in what format, when, and how often. The type of your target audience will influence this decision, as does the social media platform you use.

To gain better engagement with your content, video dominates on a couple of platforms, including Facebook, LinkedIn, and TikTok. Instagram's Reels and YouTube Shorts also perform really well. If you're considering using these platforms, lead with video content. Twitter tends to work well with images and text-based content.

In addition to content format, you also need to know what kind of content works best. One of the powerful content forms is user-generated content (UGC). The reason is that about 76% of buyers are influenced heavily by UGC rather than by influencer and brand content.

People want to know, especially about what's happening behind the scenes. For this reason, educational content is popular, particularly if you share what you do in the background. For instance, you can share how you choose a product manufacturer to ensure that your customers get quality printing and products. Claude Hopkins did this when he wanted to demonstrate the quality of Schlitz beer. When promoting Schlitz beer, Hopkins vividly described how deep the company drilled to access pure water despite having a lake nearby. Soon, Schlitz increased its market share and climbed to the second spot.

How frequently should you post? The short answer is every time you have to share news. After all, how often do TV and radio broadcast their news? Numerous times per day, and some stations focus exclusively on news. News is big business because people like to hear news to stay abreast with what's happening across the world. The good thing is that you can create and post news anytime you want, such as when introducing a new product, discounts, and competitions.

In the beginning, you can post all the other types of content two to three times a day. Watch how your audience reacts and adjust if necessary. For instance, three times might be insufficient on Twitter because people tend to post a lot more on it.

You also want to post when most of your ideal buyers are online. Otherwise, your posts could go to waste. It'll be hard to know the frequency of posting when you start. However, after a while, your data will shed light on the best days and times to post your content. Additionally, you'll know what kind of content resonates with your target audience.

Nothing prevents you from offering your products as part of your content. However, make sure that your offer is a natural result of the value-adding content you post.

Step E: Evaluate the Performance of Your Content

Social media platforms measure the performance of your content. For instance, you can check the number of comments, views, likes, clicks, and shares your content attracted on platforms like Facebook and LinkedIn. With built-in social media analytics tools, you can figure out what kind of content and posts work well with your audience.

The main use of your performance data is to help you set benchmarks per action you want. For instance, you can use previous data to calculate the average number of links clicked on posts that had them. This number can be used as a benchmark to assess the performance of future posts with links. You can do the same for shares. The reason we mention the links and shares is that they indicate that content resonates deeply with the audience, which is what you want.

Social media also gives you the option of promoting your content or brand. This is a good idea when you want to increase brand awareness. You can then run advertisements to the people who have interacted with your brand in the past.

Ultimately, you want to sell your products, which requires that you generate leads or direct purchases. That's why making offers should form part of your content plan. Other posts should offer something for free in exchange for your audience's contact information, especially their email addresses. You'll need to have an opt-in form to capture the details you want. Also, you should have the means to deliver the free thing you offer. When you have their email addresses, you can sell to them later. You can sell them over and over again.

The people who are not yet ready to buy have various reasons, including not trusting or believing in your brand. This doesn't mean they can't buy in the future, which is why you want to build a business relationship with them. There's no better method of doing so than including a plan on how to use email to convert leads into customers.

Step F: Turn Leads Into Customers

If you want to rely only on making offers on social media, it's okay. However, you'll be leaving money on the table because only those people who are ready will buy. How about those people who are higher up the marketing funnel? Some of those people could turn out to be loyal customers. If you want to nurture such people and turn them into customers, let us show you how to do so using email.

The process involves sending an email sequence consisting of nine emails; yes, just nine short emails. The fifth email is when you make an offer to your leads to buy your products. The reason it's a sequence is to allow yourself to lower your leads' buying resistance. Here are the five emails you need:

- **Email #1—Welcome email:** This email welcomes a lead who provided you with their email address in exchange for something of value you offered. In this email, you don't only welcome your lead, but you also reassure them that they've taken the right decision and tell them who you are and what you stand for. This assures them they're on the way to getting what they want. It's also in this email that you deliver what you offered if it's a digital product called a lead magnet. Go on to tell your lead what they expect in the next few days to weeks. Your aim should be to add value, culminating with making the offer.

- **Email #2—Authority-building email:** The best day to send this email is two days after the first one. With this email, your aim is to demonstrate your authority in your industry or niche. Your leads know who you are and what you stand for.

However, they wonder if you're going to help them in any way. This email provides the platform to answer that query. Your market research will come in handy. Pick one pain point related to your industry and provide a solution. This will indicate that you're an expert, and this will position you as an authority in your leads' minds.

- **Email #3—Empathy-inducing email:** While the first email reassured your leads and the second one introduced your leads' pain point and solved it, the third email aims to create a bond between you and your leads. It does this by introducing a different pain point that you went through and solved. This pain point should be the same as the one your leads are going through. For instance, perhaps in the past, they bought expensive PoD products with printing that faded during the first wash.

Empathize with them, but also show how it felt when you did the same and how you solved the problem. Automatically, as you relate your story, you'll be preparing your audience for the offer you'll be making in the next email. Also, provide your audience with content that adds value to their lives, such as a blog post or video. They don't have to be your products but should align with your brand.

- **Email #4—The offer-introducing email:** The past three emails have positioned your brand as one to trust and one that has the expertise your leads need. You've also demonstrated that you are like your leads because you've been through what they're experiencing. It's now time to make an offer that they can't turn down. Before you introduce your offer—your solution—share a story of pain and woe they probably experience and mention the solutions they tried without success.

Let them in on why the solution failed. Introduce your solution and why it works. Include proof that your solution works such as evidence from experts, academic research, celebrity, or testimonials if you have them. Include a link to your product's sales page or product description. Most importantly, make the offer available for a limited period.

- **Email #5 to email #9—Follow-up emails:** The next emails are designed to make sales follow-ups. These emails are like a salesperson. Not only should they make an offer and let it go at that. They should also follow up to convert as many leads into customers. The reason is that many people don't buy the first time they see an offer. About half of salespeople make sales follow-ups, while 4 out of 5 sales require at least 5 follow-ups. If you don't make enough follow-ups, you'll leave a ton of money on the table.

As you can see, a marketing plan focuses on the details while your marketing strategy gives a big-picture view. Depending on the number of marketing channels you want to use, you should have a marketing plan for each one of them. That's why we suggest that you start by using one marketing channel, and then add others as your business grows, and you can afford to pay for additional resources.

Step 5: Measure the Performance of Your Marketing Efforts

While the goals in your marketing plan focus on a marketing channel, the goals of your marketing strategy are global. They help you achieve your business goals. How do you know if your marketing strategy is winning? You measure the effectiveness of your marketing channels in feeding the goals of your marketing strategy. Irrespective of the kind of business you run, there are typical marketing metrics to measure, including the following:

1. **Number of customers:** The first metric to know without a doubt is the number of customers your marketing efforts have generated. This means that you should always know the sources of your customers. This is crucial because it'll help you identify more effective channels and focus more on them. Finding this

number online is easy because of the availability of website analytical tools.

2. **Number of leads generated:** Every business needs to measure the number of leads it generates over a quarter, half-yearly, and annually. Measuring this metric allows you to figure out how effective your marketing efforts are, such as social media marketing, email marketing, and content marketing. At a strategy level, you may not be interested in what marketing campaigns generate the most leads, but you do want to know the channel being used.

3. **Conversion from leads to prospects:** Not all leads become customers for various reasons. In many cases, the number of leads that don't become customers might be way larger than the number of those who do. By measuring your conversion rates from leads to customers, you can understand how hard your marketing is working. Lead conversion rate is simply the ratio of the customers generated over a given period to the number of leads generated, given as a percentage (Conversion rate = number of customers/number of leads x 100).

4. **Marketing ROI:** This metric measures how hard each dollar you invest works to generate profit. A high marketing ROI means that your investment is working far harder than when the ROI is low.

5. **Cost per lead**: It costs money to acquire leads. You want to be in control of how much you spend per lead so that you keep your marketing costs down. Also, this metric helps you figure out how effective are your marketing efforts to acquire leads. The higher this cost is, the less effective your marketing efforts

to acquire leads are. It's a great opportunity to review your copy and the kind of traffic you get.

6. **Customer acquisition cost CAC:** This is the money you spend to acquire one customer, and it's crucial to know and understand what drives it. The lower this cost is, the lower your marketing expenses will be to acquire a given number of customers. Again, this metric is great for assessing the effectiveness of your marketing.

7. **Customer lifetime value (CLV):** What do you think is responsible for building any thriving business? Why do giants like Amazon make sure that they charge reasonable prices and deliver products to their customers swiftly? The answer is a straightforward one: They want their buyers to keep coming back for more. The reason is that repeat customers cost less to get them to buy again.

Moreover, they tend to spend more, estimated to be 67% more than what new customers spend. CLV is simply what a single customer is worth to your PoD business throughout your buyer-business relationship with them. The higher it is, the more effective your customer service and allied marketing efforts are.

As you can see, it's not enough to have overall marketing goals and know what marketing channels to use. You need to measure how effective your marketing efforts are. The above metrics will get you to measure the right metrics. You can also use the above metrics to measure the effectiveness of each marketing channel that you use.

The biggest benefit of measuring the effectiveness of your marketing strategy is that you'll notice quickly if you're not executing as per your strategy.

Now, complete the checklist below to make sure you're ready to attract leads and convert them into customers cost-effectively.

Checklist

	Create a marketing strategy and include your marketing goal, marketing channels, content format, marketing budget, and marketing metrics.
	Create a marketing plan for your chosen marketing channel.
	Write an email sequence to nurture and turn leads into customers. An email sequence like this is ideal if you use search engines, pay-per-click (PPC) advertising, or social media marketing to attract leads.

Chapter 5:

Order Fulfillment and Operations

Your marketing and sales are working so well, you're generating sales every day. The products you sell are flying off your online store. It's been a lot of hard work to arrive at this stage of your business. What's going to be your most important job going forward? Your main task will be to make sure that customers get their orders in a timely manner, and they're happy. This is where you need robust order fulfillment. This chapter primarily focuses on creating such order fulfillment and supporting operations.

Understanding Order Fulfillment and Operations for a PoD Business

The order fulfillment process consists of some steps that are common irrespective of the type of fulfillment method used. For a PoD business, order fulfillment starts as soon as the customer places an order and culminates with the delivery of the product. You'll notice soon that order fulfillment is technically a customer service function because it affects the CX.

It's important for you to understand the order fulfillment process, even if you outsource, as we suggested in Chapter 3. The knowledge you gain will help you optimize your business operations, particularly customer service. With that said, here are the typical steps involved in the order fulfillment process of a PoD business:

- **Step 1: The business receives a customer's order.** The customer places an order when they have reached the purchase stage of their customer journey. This happens in your online store hosted with PoD selling platforms such as Etsy, Amazon,

Shopify, or eBay. You can also sell products directly from your own website using ecommerce online store providers such as WooCommerce. As we said earlier, it's better to use online selling platforms that integrate easily with PoD service providers like Printful and Printify.

- **Step 2: Process and verify orders.** Imagine that a customer has placed an order for a sweatshirt. Due to the failure to verify the order, you send them a hoodie. To your surprise, the customer returns the hoodie, claiming that they ordered a sweatshirt. What would you do? You can produce all the facts to prove your case, but if you don't send the customer a sweatshirt, you may lose a great customer. As you can guess, it'll be costly to your business to correct the problem. It goes without saying that you should capture such issues early. That's why you need to confirm the customer's order, including verifying billing and shipping information, the item ordered, and any other necessary details. Make sure you introduce a way for the customer to verify their order details.

- **Step 3: Your supplier prints the product.** As soon as you verify the order, it automatically reflects on your PoD service provider's order lists. Your PoD supplier has a timeline within which they'll produce the product ordered. Your customers should be aware of this to avoid problems down the line. It's usually a good idea to under-promise and over-deliver. For instance, if your supplier promises 2 days to print the customer product, you can add an extra day to cater for issues that may arise.

- **Step 4: The shipping provider delivers the product.** Companies such as Printify use third parties to deliver PoD products to customers. This means that the shipping provider will need to collect and deliver the product. But first, the products need to be packaged properly to avoid damage or shipping to the wrong customer. A shipping label should also be printed and stuck on the package. Shipping of the product can then occur.

- **Step 5: Confirm delivery of the order.** Part of customer service involves updating your customers about the status of their orders. Without this information, it's possible for the shipping provider to find no one at the shipping address provided. That's why your customers should have the means to track their orders. It's when the customer has received their product that the order fulfillment process ends.

Potential Drawbacks to the Order Fulfillment Process and How to Handle Them

Any process is bound to have issues if one or more of the steps don't proceed as planned. The order fulfillment process is no exception. There are a couple of things that can go wrong. It's crucial to find out what these are and to have solutions to address them quickly. The most common order fulfillment problems include the following.

Incorrect or Incomplete Order Information

As mentioned above, order fulfillment starts with the customer's order. During the ordering process, the customer may enter inaccurate information. For instance, they may state an incorrect product color. Another problem related to ordering might be an incorrect recording of order information. The latter can happen if you use manual systems to record customer orders. This can easily be dealt with by employing automated ordering and tracking.

There are two ways that the customer can prevent providing inaccurate or incomplete order information. They can first confirm their order details during the checkout process. Make sure that you remind your would-be customers to verify their order details before finalizing their orders.

The second opportunity for the customer to verify their order details is with an order confirmation email. It's standard practice for ecommerce merchants to send order confirmation emails to their customers soon after they've bought. Even returning customers still get these types of emails.

An order confirmation email includes the date of the order, the customer's shipping address, a description of the item ordered, billing information, shipping method, taxes charged, and the purchase total.

The good news is that the order confirmation email can be automated along with other order-related tasks. Only when the customer confirms the details of their order can the order confirmation email be sent.

There is more you can achieve with the order confirmation email. For instance, you can employ it to nurture the relationship with your customer. Many online buyers expect to receive confirmation of their orders through email. Just by sending an order confirmation email, you meet the customer's expectations. You can imagine how they'd feel if they were not to receive that kind of email! They'd probably think that you've scammed them. If you send that email, they'll be certain that their order went through successfully, and that you've gained their trust.

The order confirmation can also be used to prepare the customer for what comes next. For example, you can tell the customer when they're expected to receive their shipment. Additionally, you should inform the customer how they can track their order, how they can return the product if it's unsatisfactory, and how to contact customer support. Being open with the customer about the possibility of product return assures them it's not your intention to provide them with damaged or incorrect merchandise. How can a customer who has been prepared that way mistrust your PoD business?

Informing the customer what to expect after making the order and providing the next steps minimizes the need for customer support. This sets your customer support free from handling an excessive number of support calls.

If you have other products you're selling, an order confirmation email is a great tool to offer them. Without a doubt, if you offer products that complement what the customer is buying, some of them will buy.

As a result, an order confirmation email can bump up your average order size.

All the benefits of sending order confirmation emails can go to waste if you don't send them timely. Ideally, you want to send these emails a few minutes, if not seconds, after the customer makes the purchase. Furthermore, make sure that your order confirmation emails are mobile-friendly, considering that mobile devices have become popular means for checking emails.

Product Printing Delays

One of the disadvantages of a PoD business is that it has no control over the manufacturing of the products it sells. The overarching benefit is that it doesn't have to invest in costly production machinery. Just imagine what type of machines you'd need to purchase if you manufacture your products yourself!

However, this doesn't mean that your supplier won't have issues with producing your products. The issues can range from finding the right raw material to print delays due to the inevitable breakdown of printers.

When looking for a PoD supplier, you need to make sure they can communicate such issues in a timely manner. Best of all, consider using a supplier who has backup in case of delays. For instance, they can contract other suppliers to come in during difficult times and take over manufacturing temporarily.

To be on the safe side, always communicate with your customers when there are such issues. If it comes to a push, purchase similar items from another supplier and get them delivered to your customers. Perhaps this problem suggests that you should have more than one PoD service provider. When one of them can't manufacture your products, you can use the other ones.

Another method of handling production delays is by using order tracking software. These systems monitor and track the progress of an order from start to end. With 97% of customers expecting to track their orders, you won't have to inform them that there's a problem. What you'd focus on is ensuring that you turn the bad experience into a wonderful opportunity—an opportunity to demonstrate how well you handle difficulties.

Shipping Delays

Shipping delays are like being held in transit during rush hour or train delay. No one likes to be stuck on their way to their destination. A customer waiting to receive their product is the same—they want to receive their product on time. Every merchant should have systems in place to ensure their customers' shipping expectations aren't shattered.

Just imagine how your customers, who're used to receiving their products in days, have to wait for weeks! You can be sure that such customers will be disappointed. Unfortunately, this can quickly escalate into frustration. Unless you do something about shipping delays, you might start experiencing higher rates of cart abandonment. You might also lose some of your regular customers, which will hurt your revenues and profit margins.

There are numerous causes of shipping delays.

1. **Supply issues:** One of the reasons is supply chain disruptions. For instance, if there are delays in the delivery of raw materials, your PoD service supplier can't manufacture your products. Unfortunately, there's little you can do about such delays. Your best bet is to have a backup supplier. If that fails, you can set up your ecommerce store so that immediately after there are supply chain issues, you take the products affected out of stock. Keep your eye on your supply chain, and immediately communicate with customers and suppliers to resolve these issues faster.

2. **Incorrect shipping address:** We've dealt with this earlier. As mentioned there, your best bet is to allow the customer to confirm their order details. If they do this, and you still experience shipping address issues, you may need to find another way.

3. **Carrier problems:** Shipping delays may be caused by problems on the carrier side. For instance, they may experience vehicle breakdowns. Your best bet is to use a reputable carrier that has a high level of customer service. You expect that when there are carrier problems that affect your customer orders, you're informed immediately. Additionally, that information must filter to the customer right away.

Ineffective Quality Control

No customer wants to receive a damaged product, especially after waiting for it for days. It can be even more frustrating if the customer receives the wrong product. Whether it happens by mistake or otherwise, it's unacceptable to deliver a customer's product in poor condition.

Not only does this deliver a poor CX, but it also costs you money. If you ship a damaged product, you'll need to replace it, which means you buy the same item twice. Increased costs escalate your cost of goods sold (COGS) and reduce your profit margin. You should avoid sending damaged products to your customers at all costs. If it means taking an extra 5 min to double-check the quality of the product before shipping it, go ahead and do it. The cost of losing customers is too much to take for granted. Worse, they can influence others to stay away from your store like a plague.

After taking extra care to deliver good quality products, you may have one or two of such issues. In that case, replace the damaged item for free, including return of the damaged product and shipping of the new one.

Inventory Management Failure

You're probably wondering why this guide discusses inventory management when you don't keep stock. Your PoD service provider or their vendor does keep inventory. How they manage that inventory can impact your order fulfillment process. If your service provider doesn't have inventory, your customer will not receive their product.

Inventory management is part of supply management, but we wanted to discuss it separately because of its importance. A PoD supplier that fails to keep inventory at the required levels can cause you to miss sales. Imagine the size of the impact on revenue if this happens when demand for your products is high! Inevitably, your business will lose a lot of money and find it difficult to recover. What's worse is that when customers realize that you don't have stock, they buy from your competitors. As such, when your competitors thrive, you'll struggle. By the time you recover, you'll likely have lost market share.

Yes, you don't have inventory to directly manage, but it's necessary to keep track of inventory regularly. A good PoD supplier will update you on the level of inventory regularly, such as daily. Of course, you should agree with your supplier on what minimum inventory to keep. As soon as the inventory level dips, you may begin to prepare to kick in your backup.

In the final analysis, you need to analyze every step of the order fulfillment process. This will help you identify issues quickly and proactively address them. For instance, if your supplier keeps messing up inventory levels, you can look for a different one. Even if there are no issues when you analyze your order fulfillment process, you'll still likely find improvement opportunities.

How to Optimize Order Fulfillment Operations

Ideally, every retail business wants to have an error-free order fulfillment process. It's unfortunate that there are going to be mistakes in one or more steps of this vital operation. This shouldn't be a surprise because if something can go wrong, it will at some point. Your best bet is to get as close as possible to optimum order fulfillment operations. This requires continuous improvement. How do you go about this optimization process? Let's find out.

It's understandable that your order fulfillment operations may not be optimal from the beginning. You'll probably be fighting fires in the early days of your business before you stabilize your operations. Reaching stability doesn't mean that you can't do better than that because there's always room for improvement in any process. Before you begin optimizing, you need to decide why you're doing it, which is where optimization goals come in.

Before setting optimization goals, take stock of your current order fulfillment performance. If you don't yet have an order fulfillment system to measure and track your performance, research and decide on one. Your supplier can provide the information you need from their order fulfillment system.

Some of the most important order fulfillment metrics to track include the following:

- **Customer satisfaction:** This is the ratio of the number of satisfied customers to the total number of customers who gave you feedback about their satisfaction levels. Calculate this key performance indicator over a given period of time, such as monthly or quarterly. You can find the numbers you want by asking the customers to give feedback about their order shipping experience.

- **Order accuracy rate:** This is the percentage of orders fulfilled without errors such as damaged products or missing items. You can calculate it by dividing the number of accurate orders by the total number of orders dispatched and expressing the result as a percentage.

- **Delivery time:** This is the time from when the delivery vehicle leaves the packing facility to when it reaches the customer. It doesn't matter what type of vehicle your carrier uses to ship your customers' orders. Data to determine your delivery time should be available from your carrier's shipping and logistics software.

- **On-time shipping rate:** Are you shipping your orders on time? The quickest way to know is to check your on-time shipping rate. Divide the number of orders shipped on time by the total number of orders shipped over the same period, and multiply the result by 100. The higher this number is, the better your on-time shipping rates are.

- **Order processing time:** Closely allied with the on-time shipping rate is the order processing time. This is the time it takes from when your customer places an order to when it gets shipped. Customers want their orders shipped quickly, meaning that the longer your order processing time is, the higher the chances of making lower revenues. Divide the total time spent processing orders by the number of orders over the same period.

- **Order return rate:** This is the percentage of orders that your customers returned for whatever reason. Returns may be associated with refunds, which will negatively impact your revenues and profit margins. A high order return rate should be a cause for concern and needs to be addressed swiftly. You determine it by dividing the number of orders returned by the total number of orders delivered and multiplying the result by 100.

- **Rate of damage-free orders customers receive:** This measure helps figure out the rate at which you deliver undamaged orders to your customers. It should be as high as possible, close to 100% if your quality control is top-notch. To determine this metric, divide the number of damage-free orders by the total orders delivered over the period of interest and multiply the answer by 100.

- **Order fill rate:** This metric helps you determine how effectively your service provider manages the inventory of your products. If they're on top of the order fill rate, orders will be fulfilled nearly always from available stock. Order fill rate is the ratio of the number of orders shipped to the number of orders placed, expressed as a percentage.

- **Average cost per order:** This is the cost you incur to fulfill a single order over a given period. You obtain it by dividing the total order fulfillment cost by the number of orders fulfilled over the period in question.

The above sample of metrics may seem daunting at first. However, when you look at the measures closely, it's worth tracking and knowing them. Using inventory management software will simplify tracking and analyzing them.

Establish Your Major Order Fulfillment Optimization Goals

As you saw above, the order fulfillment process can have numerous metrics to determine its effectiveness. For optimization purposes, it'll be too much to improve all of them at once; you should focus on a few critical ones. Since customer satisfaction is one of the critical order fulfillment metrics, it's worth including it. Consider others you feel should be optimized.

Establishing the metrics to improve should be easy. All it takes is finding out what the industry benchmarks are or where industry leaders operate. Then you compare those performances with your own performances. The metrics that need optimization will be obvious, saving you from the agony of choosing the ones closest to your heart.

Once you have chosen the metrics to optimize and know the current levels, ask yourself where you want to take them. For instance, if your current delivery time is between 3 and 5 days, you may set the goal of getting it down to between 2 and 4 days. Approach the other metrics of interest the same way. When done, you'll be having your order fulfillment goals. Remember that every goal you set should pass the SMART test.

Map Out the Steps That Produce Each Metric

It's now time to figure out the weaknesses that lead to the results you're currently achieving. This is crucial because without knowing what's holding your order fulfillment back, you can't address it. Luckily, each result you're achieving consists of steps, and you can find what these are.

The easiest method to determine the steps that produce a certain order fulfillment result is to map it out. An example of how to do this will be helpful.

Suppose that one of the metrics you want to improve is the order processing time. You first need to find out what happens once a customer has placed their order. Here are the steps for a PoD business:

- Step 1: The order automatically goes to your PoD service provider.

- Step 2: The PoD service provider prints the design onto the product according to the design you provided.

- Step 3: Your vendor quality checks the printing and the product.

- Step 4: The product gets packaged and labeled for shipping.

- Step 5: The carrier collects the product for delivery.

- Step 6: Your customer receives their order.

It's crucial to capture all the steps involved. Don't worry at this point about how well each step is accomplished. That time will come.

Evaluate Each Step Mapped

The next phase of order fulfillment optimization is analyzing each step of the process you want to optimize. Taking the example above, you'll analyze the steps that handle the product, meaning Steps 2 through 6. This means understanding what happens at each step and how long it takes.

Step 6 should be quick because it requires the customer's confirmation that they received the package without any damage; your carrier's records will have this information. If there were no issues with the package, the damage would not have occurred when the order was in transit.

You then evaluate Step 5 and continue that way until the first step. You're surely going to find that one or more of the steps contributed to or caused the damage. Once you find such steps, you need to work out their weaknesses and address them as soon as possible. Test your solutions to make sure that they don't introduce problems you never thought about.

Evaluate the Effectiveness of Your Solutions

How do you know if the improvements you've implemented have delivered the results you want? You keep measuring the metrics you're interested in. If over a reasonable time period, you get the desired results, you turn the new process into an SOP.

The challenge with PoD businesses when addressing order fulfillment processes is that you work with and through third parties. It's likely they will need to improve and optimize their processes. However, you can't stand and watch when your business suffers due to third-party operations. You intervene and even give an ultimatum that if they don't improve, you'll move your business elsewhere.

Remember also that no process is 100% efficient. There's always something you can do to improve your order fulfillment to near ideal. So, make continuous improvement part of your value systems.

Now, complete the action described in the checklist below to ensure that you optimize your order fulfillment process.

Checklist

	Identifying and measure order fulfillment metrics that inform your performance such as customers satisfaction, delivery time, order return rate, and order fill-rate.
	Monitor improvements that you've implemented to see how effective your efforts are, and adjust your strategy from those findings.

Chapter 6:

Financial Management and Planning

How does a business, small or large, fail even if it generates a lot of profit? The answer lies in the failure to manage cash—a lack of sound financial management. How can you cover the costs of your business if you don't have cash? You can't, and your best bet will be to close the doors. You can have one of the best PoD businesses in the world and still fail.

It's no accident that you need to make crucial financial decisions right from the start of your PoD business. Otherwise, you can easily misallocate the money that comes in and run into financial problems. Doing this is even more crucial for anyone who has never managed business finance before. That's why we'll begin this chapter by covering the fundamentals of business finance.

Why You Need Sound Small Business Financial Management

When you're well acquainted with your business finances, you'll gain crucial benefits other than having the cash for daily operations and marketing. This makes financial management a key aspect of business success. The financial condition of your business influences the decisions you make. For instance, you may need to crack down on your sales when you foresee troubles ahead. Here are other advantages of business financial management:

1. **It helps with tax planning.** Every business that makes a profit is required to pay income taxes. Typically, the higher the profit your business makes, the higher the income tax you will pay.

When you manage your business finances well, you'll arrange your activities so that you only pay the tax that's due—you don't overpay or underpay. Most importantly, you can plan your taxes in such a way that you enhance the growth of your business.

2. **The business owner can allocate funds effectively.** As a PoD business owner, you manufacture, sell products, and retain customers for as long as you can. You repeat this cycle again and again to grow your business. Every part of this cycle costs money, which requires efficient allocation of those funds. You need to pay your suppliers in a timely manner and if you have employees, pay their salaries on time. This requires having cash, making it necessary to be astute with your business finances.

3. **It helps with handling financial rough times.** All businesses experience good and bad economic times. When times are good, you can get away with financial mismanagement. However, when tough times come—and they do come—improper financial management will land your business in trouble. In some cases, you might be forced to close down if you can't quickly raise the funds you need. With sound financial management, you'll know that tough times need cash and save enough during the good times. Even when you want to scale your business, you won't have to borrow to do so.

4. **Sound financial management helps measure ROI.** When you start a PoD or any type of business, you're investing. The purpose of any investment is to get the best return possible. How would you know what this return is if you don't maintain sound financial management principles? You can't. Calculation of ROI requires financial data, which, in turn, is an outcome of proper financial management. The reports generated from financial management don't only help with ROI calculation, but also with tax determinations.

From the foregoing, it's clear that you can't skimp on your business' financial management. Nothing beats having the right processes and financial management tools. Most importantly, you, as the business owner, need to have a basic understanding of business finance. The next section will help you fill this gap if you don't come from a finance background.

Understanding Your Business Finances

Business finance involves doing tasks such as bookkeeping and filing taxes that are often performed by accounting professionals. These tasks are so crucial because you need to pay the right amount of taxes instead of overpaying. If you overpay, Uncle Sam (the taxman) would be excited, but your business may be stretched financially.

One of the most important accounting tasks is accurate financial planning. This involves forecasting your revenues, expenses, and the cash flow status of your PoD business over a given period. Following financial planning comes the task of managing your finances, which includes record keeping, financial reporting, and the management of expenses and cash. Projecting your business' finances requires an understanding of the three basic financial statements.

Three Basic Financial Statements

Financial planning relies heavily on the projected inflow and outflow of funds from your business. There are three types of financial statements that you need to understand for accurate financial planning. They are the income or profit and loss statement, cash flow statement, and balance sheets.

Income Statement

This is a financial statement that shows the profit and loss of a business over a given time period, usually a quarter or year. For accurate calculation of the profit or loss, it's necessary to know your revenues and expenses.

An income statement captures your revenue, costs to generate the revenue, gross profit, expenses such as administrative and selling, other costs and income, tax expenses, interest expenses, and earnings of net profit. The data used to compile the income statement doesn't rely on any information from other financial statements. That's why it's the first financial statement to understand and create.

It follows that you need to understand these accounting terms for accurate communication and financial reporting. Let's break down the structure and components of a typical income statement. Let's assume that this statement covers the period of a year.

- **Revenue:** The first item in an income statement is the revenue, also called sales in some businesses. This is the total dollar value of the items you sold to generate business income. If you've sold 5,000 mugs for $15 an item over a year, your revenue will be 5,000 x $15 = $75,000. If you sell multiple types of PoD products, your revenue will be the sum of the total income from each type of item sold.

- **COGS:** This is the cost incurred to produce and sell your products to generate revenue. For a PoD business, this cost includes printing and production of your merchandise. If it costs $5 to produce 1 mug in the example above, your COGS will be 5,000 x $5 = $25,000.

- **Gross profit:** This component evaluates the efficiency of the production of merchandise. The higher it is, the better you are at controlling the cost of producing your goods. You obtain gross profit by deducting COGS from revenue. In the example above, your gross profit will be $75,000 – $25,000 = $50,000.

- **Selling expenses:** These costs are incurred to advertise and promote your goods. If you spend 12% of your revenue on this expense, your selling costs will be $75,000 x .12 = $9,000. Of course, you want it to be as low as possible.

- **General and administrative (G&A) expenses:** These are costs incurred to run your business. For a PoD business, some of these costs include accounting expenses, insurance products, office expenses, and your salary if you draw any. For this example, we'll assume this cost is $4,000. The sum of selling and G&A expenses is called operating costs.

- **Earnings before interest, tax, depreciation, and amortization (EBITDA):** This is the profit you generate before deducting interest on loans (if any), taxes, depreciation, and amortization. You get it by subtracting total operating expenses from the gross profit. Moving along with our example, EBITDA will be $50,000 − $9,000 − $4,000 = $37,000.

- **Depreciation and amortization expense:** It costs money to purchase capital assets such as computers, printers, vehicles, and furniture. These assets are used to generate revenue. The cost of acquiring these assets is spread over a number of years. These noncash expenses are called depreciation. While depreciation applies to tangible assets, amortization does the same regarding intangible assets.

- **Operating income:** Accountants call this component earnings before interest and taxes (EBIT). It tells you how much profit or loss you generated from your business operations. This income excludes any expense or income unrelated to business operations. You calculate it by subtracting operating, depreciation, and amortization expenses. Let's assume that the depreciation expense of your PoD business over the year of interest is $300. In the example begun above, EBIT will be $37,000 − $300 = $36,700.

- **Interest expense:** This is the expense incurred due to borrowing funds. If you charge your business interest for the initial investment you make in it, your company's income statement will have interest expense. Otherwise, if your business doesn't borrow money from anyone, there won't be this component in your company's income statement. Let's assume you don't charge interest on the money you use to launch your PoD business.

- **Other expenses:** PoD businesses may incur fulfillment costs if their customers don't pay for shipping and handling. Waving this cost may attract customers to your business, but lower your profits. Let's assume that you don't incur any fulfillment expenses.

- **Pre-tax income:** Also called earnings before tax (EBT), this component of the income statement tells you how much profit you've made after subtracting all the expenses mentioned above. Said another way, it's the money that remains after subtracting interest expense and other expenses from operating income. In our case, you don't have the interest expense and other expenses, meaning that your pre-tax income is the same as your operating income, which is $36,700.

- **Income taxes:** The amount of tax you pay depends on the legal type of your company. On average, small businesses pay around 19.8% of their pre-tax income annually. Using this figure in our above example, your income tax for the year under consideration will be $7,266.60.

- **Net income or earnings:** If you've ever heard about the bottom line in business, this is the metric referred to. It tells you whether you've made a profit or loss, which is why the income statement is also called the profit and loss statement. In the example we've been dealing with, your net income will be $29,433.40.

That's all there is to the income statement. We can summarize the annual income statement we generated in table form as follows:

The Unique Accessories Company Income Statement For the year ended February 28	
Revenue	$75,000
Cost of goods sold	$25,000
Gross profit	$50,000
Selling expenses	$9,000
G&A expenses	$4,000
Total operating expenses	$13,000
EBITDA	$37,000
Depreciation expense	$300
Amortization expense	$0
Operating income	$36,700
Interest expense	$0
Other expenses	$0
Pre-tax income or EBT	$36,700
Income taxes	$7,266.60
Net income or earnings	**$29,433.40**

The above income statement reports what profit or loss you made in the previous year. How do you predict your profit or losses when you start your PoD business? This is a wonderful question because you want to catch profit issues early, not when the whole year is gone.

That's where projecting your income and expenses prior to starting your PoD business comes in handy. So, how do you go about doing this? We'll cover how to forecast your finances after discussing the other two financial statements.

Cash Flow Statement

While the income statement measures the revenues, expenses, and profitability of your business, it says nothing about the movement of cash. If you relied only on the income statement to run your business, you could wind up having a profit but no cash. The reason is that profit isn't equal to cash. You don't pay your suppliers with profit but with cash. As such, you need to manage your business' cash carefully.

A business' cash management begins by preparing a cash flow statement. This is a financial statement that measures the inflow and outflow of cash over a given period, typically a year. Your company's net cash position gives you its financial health. It's easy to prepare a cash flow statement by using small business accounting software. But first, it's essential to understand the cash flow statement.

There are three key components of a cash flow statement: cash flow from operating activities, investing activities, and financing activities. Let's learn what each of these elements is about.

- **Cash flow from operating activities:** As you probably noted from the income statement, cash is involved in running your core business activities. That cash also appears in the cash flow statement as net income. This means that the cash that comes in as revenue and that which goes out as expenses is accounted for in the cash flow statement.

- **Cash flow from investing activities:** What happens when your business keeps generating profits year in and year out? It's likely that you may invest some of it in assets such as real estate or buy business assets such as vehicles. When you dispose of these assets, your business generates cash. This kind of cash is said to be cash flow from investing activities. Other kinds of cash generated this way may be rental or licensing income.

- **Cash flow from financing activities:** This is the cash generated from investors or financiers and also dividend payments. Interest expenses also form part of this kind of cash because it originates from financing activities.

Five Steps of Preparing a Cash Flow Statement

Even if you might opt to work with an accountant or use accounting software, it's still advisable to understand how to prepare a cash flow statement. Doing so will help you understand the numbers you see in your cash flow statement. This is nonnegotiable for savvy business financial management. Here are the steps for preparing a cash flow statement.

1. **Figure out the starting cash balance.** The starting cash balance is the cash available at the beginning of a period, such as a year. It's the same figure as the ending cash balance of the preceding cash flow statement covering the same period. What will this figure be for a startup in its first year? It will simply be the amount you invest to get your business started.

2. **Calculate the cash flow from operations.** There are two ways of calculating this figure: the indirect and the direct methods. The indirect method uses the net income from the income statement as the starting balance of your cash flow statement. However, you'll need to add back depreciation and amortization because they're noncash expenses.

   In contrast, the direct method calculates the starting balance by subtracting all cash disbursements from the total cash collected from options. Using the indirect method is quicker because most of the data used is available from the income statement and the balance sheet. Whichever method you use, the result will be the same.

3. **Determine cash flow from investing activities.** This section captures all the cash generated and spent to acquire long-term assets such as equipment and property. Remember that long-term assets can be used for more than a year. A vehicle or

computer is a good example of a long-term asset. No debt should be included in calculating cash flow from activities.

4. **Figure out cash flow from financing activities.** This part of the cash flow statement captures all the cash inflows and outflows associated with raising cash and paying it back. If you've loaned your business money or invested in it, that figure should appear here.

5. **Calculate the ending balance.** This step for preparing the cash flow statement is to calculate the ending balance of cash during the reporting period. This figure is simply the sum of all the cash flows calculated above, including the starting balance.

You should also be interested in a metric called the change in net cash. This is the sum of cash flows from the three types of business activities defined above. It tells you whether you've added or removed cash from the business over the reporting period. If the change in net cash is positive, your business has brought in more cash than it took out, which is a good thing. On the other hand, a negative change in net cash indicates that your business used more cash than it generated over the reporting period.

Example of a cash flow statement for a PoD business that is preparing this kind of financial statement for the first time.

Please note: The numbers used in the example financial statements below are for illustration purposes only. They're not actual numbers.

The Unique Accessories Company Income Statement For the year ended February 28	
Starting balance	$0
Cash flows from operating activities	

Net income	$29,433.40
Adjustments to reconcile net income to net cash from operating activities:	
Depreciation and amortization	$300
Changes in current assets and liabilities:	
Decrease in prepaid expenses	$0
Decrease in accounts payable	$0
Net cash from operating activities	**$29,733.40**
Cash flows from investing activities	
Capital expenditure	($450)
Net cash from investing activities	**($450)**
Cash flows from financing activities	
Equity financing	$5,000
Dividends paid	($2,000)
Net cash from financing activities	**$3,000**
Net increase in cash during the year	**$32,733.40**
Cash at the end of the year	**$32,733.40**

Do you notice that, for this company, the bottom line or net profit isn't the same as net cash flow at the end of the year? Net profit is all to do with cash flows from operating activities, while net cash flow is a function of all expenses related to your entire business activities.

For this business, there should have been $32,733.40 sitting in the bank. This figure will be the starting balance for the following year's cash flow statement.

Balance Sheet

The third basic financial statement is the balance sheet, also called the statement of financial position. Have you ever heard about net worth in personal finance? If you did, be aware that a balance sheet is a tool to measure the net worth of your business. In case you haven't heard about net worth, don't worry, you'll still understand the balance as we go over it below.

In a balance sheet, a business records its assets, liabilities, and owner's equity at a given point in time. Before we proceed, how about clarifying the meaning of assets, liabilities, and owner's equity?

- **Assets:** Things, tangible and intangible, that your business owns.

- **Liabilities:** Things that your business owes, such as a loan.

- **Owner's equity:** The amount belonging to investors in the business after deducting liabilities.

How does a balance sheet help you as a business owner? Just as you go to a physician to check your health, a balance sheet helps you determine the financial health of your business. It's even more important when used with income and cash flow statements. You can use the balance for the following:

- **Leverage:** This term explains how much debt you have compared to what you own. The balance sheet helps you understand your business' financial risk. You can do this by comparing your debts to owner's equity. If the debt is too high relative to the owner's equity, you can take steps to fix the issue that's causing that high leverage.

- **Liquidity:** The word "liquidity" refers to how quickly you can convert an asset into cash. The most liquid asset is cash, which is why having cash is crucial when you run a business. By comparing short-term assets to short-term liabilities, you can figure out the liquidity of your business. If short-term assets far exceed short-term liabilities, you should cover your short-term debts relatively easier.

- **Efficiency:** The purpose of your business' assets is to generate revenue. A business that efficiently uses its assets will generate a lot more revenue per dollar of its assets. The balance sheet calculates the value of your assets to allow you to determine how efficiently they deliver revenue.

Now that you know how beneficial the balance sheet is to your business, let's closely look at this financial statement.

The balance sheet consists of the following items:

- **Assets:** This section captures all the things that your business owns. These items are listed from the most liquid to the least liquid. Assets are divided into current assets and long-term assets.

   ○ **Current assets:** They can be converted into cash in a year or less. These include cash and cash equivalents, marketable securities such as shares and bonds, accounts receivable, inventory, and prepaid expenses. Accounts receivable is what others owe you for buying on credit. If you sell for cash, this item won't be included in your balance sheet.

   ○ **Long-term assets:** These are assets that can't be turned into cash in one year. They include fixed assets such as computers, machinery, and real estate property; long-term securities to be liquidated after a year; and intangible assets such as patents, copyrights, and trademarks.

- **Liabilities:** This is the second major section of a balance sheet and captures what you owe to others. It's divided into short- and long-term liabilities. Short-term liabilities include payroll, taxes, utilities, and regular payments you make toward long-term debts. Long-term liabilities cover debts such as deferred income taxes and long-term loans. A PoD business grown organically shouldn't have long-term liabilities if run properly.

- **Owner's equity:** This section lists money that belongs to shareholders, which is why it's also called shareholders' equity. Any money you invested into the business is part of the owner's equity. It may also include money the business reinvests for growth purposes. To determine the owner's equity, subtract total liabilities from total assets.

How to Prepare a Balance Sheet

You may not be an accountant, but it helps to understand how to prepare a balance sheet. One big reason is that you'll understand how to use it better than a business owner who can't read it well. Here's how to go about compiling a balance sheet:

- **Step 1—Select the balance sheet date:** Typical dates for preparing balance sheets are monthly, quarterly, half-yearly, and yearly. You have a choice about the frequency of preparing your balance sheets. However, make sure that you also include the end-of-the-year one.

- **Step 2—Identify all your assets:** Figure out what assets your business owns. List them from the most liquid to the least liquid. If you have cash, it will be at the top of your list. It's helpful to use a spreadsheet because it simplifies this task. It's even better if you separate your short-term from long-term assets. Make sure that you include noncurrent assets such as your designs to your list of long-term assets.

- **Step 3—Calculate the total of all your assets:** Determine the sum of all your current assets as well as the total of your long-term assets. Now, add up the two figures to find the sum of all of your assets. This figure is your total assets.

- **Step 4—Calculate total liabilities:** Follow Steps 2 and 3 regarding liabilities to calculate the total liabilities.

- **Step 5—Determine owner's equity:** Owner's equity can be obtained directly by adding retained earnings to share capital. Retained earnings are the money that the business retains after paying out dividends. Don't confuse this money with the salary that you may draw from your business. That should be part of your operational expenses. Share capital is money you raise by issuing shares to someone else. If you're the sole owner, the money you invested entitles you to all your company's shares.

- **Step 6—Sum your total liabilities to owner's equity:** This calculation aims to check if the numbers you've used in preparing the balance sheet are accurate. If all is well, total liabilities plus owner's equity should equal total assets. In case this isn't so, review your calculations.

Preparing a balance sheet may sound complicated. It isn't if you know and apply the proper accounting rules and procedures. We won't go into this since it's beyond the scope of this guide.

There's a connection between the income statement and the balance sheet. For example, interest expense appears as a liability on the balance sheet and revenue is linked with cash—an asset. Ideally, you should prepare the balance sheet after you've created the income statement. Here's an example of the balance sheet:

The Unique Accessories Company Income Statement For the year ended February 28			
ASSETS		**LIABILITIES**	
Current assets		**Current liabilities**	
Cash	$32,733.40	Tax payable	$7,266.60
Prepaid insurance	$1,000	**Total current liabilities**	
Total current assets	**$33,733.40**	**Long-term liabilities**	
Long-term assets		**Total long-term liabilities**	$0
Equipment	$450	**Total liabilities**	$7,266.60
Accumulated depreciation	($300)	**SHAREHOLDERS' EQUITY**	
Total long-term assets	**$150**	Equity capital	$5,000
Intangible assets		Retained earnings	$29,433.40
Trade names	$5,000	**Total shareholders' equity**	**$34,433.40**
Goodwill	$2,000		
Total	**$7,000**		

intangible assets			
Other assets	$816.60		
Total assets	$41,700	**Total liabilities and shareholders' equity**	$41,700

That's all there is to preparing a balance for your PoD business. It might look intimidating at first, but after going over it a couple of times, it'll become easier to read and understand. Most importantly, the knowledge you gain can be used to analyze any balance sheet.

Don't worry if preparing the above three financial statements sounds complicated. There's an alternative to creating them yourself: You can use accounting software.

Why Choose Accounting Software?

The creation of accounting software has made the difficult task of small business finance easier. It was created to eliminate the manual task of performing tasks such as preparing financial reports. This is having a huge positive impact on the productivity of owners of small businesses. Back then, only giant corporations had the ability to perform accounting functions quickly. Today, you too can do so.

Accounting software is simply a tool that consists of numerous applications for recording, storing, and summarizing financial data for business decision-making. Some of the notable functions of this type of software include invoicing, quotation creation, business budgeting, and financial reporting. Gone are the days of spending days preparing financial statements. Instead of seeing your company's financial statements once a year, you can check them as and when you want. There are many other benefits of using accounting software, including these:

1. **Enhanced accuracy of your financial information.** If you've ever worked with a lot of numerical data, you know how easy it is to make errors. This used to be a common occurrence in business accounting until accounting software surfaced. Back then, you could capture a lot of data only to discover later that you made big errors. With accounting software, you can generate multiple financial pieces of information that are error-free as long as you enter the raw data accurately. This is because you can generate information such as financial statements without having to work on them directly. The software automates the whole process, which improves accuracy.

2. **Helps simplify the development and growth of your business.** Managing your finances ranks high, and it should, among your business activities. Creating and managing budgets can be time-consuming. This will not be the case anymore when you use accounting software. You can check the health of your business anytime and make sure that funds are directed where they should go. You can also run "what if" scenarios to anticipate future financial needs and be prepared if you need to source additional funds. As such, accounting software can come in handy in developing and growing your PoD business.

3. **It improves productivity.** Because accounting software improves accuracy, it minimizes the need for rework. Furthermore, it allows you to do more accounting work than you would if you handled business finances manually. With improved productivity comes time savings. For instance, you won't have to manually prepare financial statements as the software will handle this automatically.

4. **It helps you stay on top of tax compliance.** Paperwork is one of the stressors of small business owners. Accounting software minimizes the time to prepare your business tax returns. Some accounting software applications include automated record-keeping and tax-specific functions. You won't have to manually track the income and expenses necessary for filing tax returns. Estimating your tax liabilities

becomes simpler with accounting software featuring a tax calculator and planner. When ready, you may add an automated tax-filing feature, adding to your convenience.

Like all types of software, accounting software applications can only be effective provided you feed it with accurate finance data. You may have heard about a software principle that says, "Garbage in, garbage out." If you enter inaccurate financial data into accounting software, you'll base your business decisions on wrong information. As such, you won't move your business in the direction you desire.

Entering financial data and preparing various financial reports fall into a discipline known as bookkeeping. When you have accounting software, you won't have to hire a bookkeeper, saving you thousands of dollars per year. You can also access the accounting software anywhere you are if you choose an online version. Accounting software comes in handy when you want to prepare your business' financial projections, a topic you're ready to learn now.

How to Prepare Your Startup's Financial Projections

There's no financial management unless you first create a financial plan. This is the task we're now going to tackle head-on—a task that may sound daunting if you're not an accountant. We can assure you that if you follow how to create the three basic financial statements discussed above, you can prepare financial projections.

A financial projection is a budget you use to forecast future business revenue and expenses. It's a vital tool to have when planning your startup. You don't want to put in a huge effort in building a business that has no charge of generating the revenue and profit you want.

Typical financial projections cover both the short- and long-term. Short-term projections cover a year of operations and include a month-to-month breakdown of income and expenses. For longer periods, you use long-term projections.

Note that a startup relies heavily on data and facts available in the market. When you're done creating financial projections, you should have a projected income statement, balance sheet, and cash flow statement.

There are numerous benefits to doing financial projections. For a startup, these projections will help you figure out if you'll get back your money with profit. Remember that inflation eats the value of the dollar. This means that a dollar you have today is worth more than the one you earn in the future. Your current money should work harder to keep up with the pace of inflation, plus bring in more profit.

We've mentioned earlier that cash flow contributes to the failure of many small businesses. Part of the problem is that small business owners don't do financial projections and run out of cash when they shouldn't. For example, they may run out of money when they have to pay key suppliers. Financial projections show when you're likely to run out of cash, which gives you ample time to find the cash hole. For instance, you could change production plans or pricing at the right time. Alternatively, but not exclusively, you can change your capital expenditure decisions.

As your PoD business grows, you'll probably need to hire additional employees. How are you going to know when to do this if you don't do financial projections? It's going to be hard, which is why some business owners opt to hire extra employees in a hurry. No wonder they hire the wrong type of employees.

There might come a time when you want to exit your business by selling it. We hope you don't reach a point when you do this, but circumstances can force you to. How are you going to price your company? This is another area where you'll need financial projections, just as stock market investors often do.

Steps for Creating Financial Projections

Now that you've seen the benefits of having financial projections, it's time to prepare them. It takes five steps as discussed below.

126

Step 1: Estimate Your Future Sales

The projections you prepare should be monthly for the 1st year, quarterly for the following year, and annually for the next 3 years. This means that your projections will cover a period of 5 years.

The first element to estimate is your sales. You need to answer the question, "What will drive my sales?" For every online business, the source of sales will be the visitors to your online store. You're either going to drive these people to your store organically or through paid initiatives. Whatever source you use, you should know how many people visit your store monthly.

The next thing to figure out is how many of those people will convert into customers. A bit of research will help you figure out what that conversion rate should be. If you sell clothing, you may expect conversion rates of between 1.01% to 2.20%. So, if you sell T-shirts, you'll sell 1 or 2 shirts for every 100 visitors to your online store. Let's say that you drive 5,000 visitors to your online store each month. The number of buyers will be 50 (5,000 x 1.01% = 50.5), rounded down.

Let's further estimate that the number of customers who return the T-shirts they bought is 20%. This means that you'll remain with 40 buyers (50 x .80 = 40). If the T-shirt sells for $30 apiece, your monthly revenue will be $1,200 or $14,400 annually if you keep selling 40 shirts per month.

For the second year, estimate the increase in sales you want to generate to work out your quarterly sales. Follow the same thinking when forecasting your sales in the third year going forward. Remember that your current year's estimates will always be monthly.

Once again, note once more that the data used in the examples above are for illustration only.

Step 2: Project Expenses

The second step is to estimate your expenses. You'll recall from our discussion of the income statement that your expenses include COGS and operating expenses. COGS consists of costs associated with producing the products you sell, which include product costs, merchant fees, fulfillment costs, and customer service.

The simplest method of working out COGS is as a percentage of revenue because PoD businesses don't keep inventory. Let's assume that the gross profit of your type of business is 60%. You'll need to research what typical gross profits are as a percentage of revenue for your kind of business. This suggests that COGS is 40% of revenue. Thus, for the scenario described in Step 1 above, COGS will be $480 per month or $5,760 per year.

Use the same idea as above to calculate operating expenses such as marketing, advertising, salaries (if any), selling platform subscriptions, and insurance. Don't forget to estimate the depreciation and amortization expenses as well as tax expenses. Check the example income statement discussed earlier for all the expenses you need to figure out.

To avoid underestimating your projections, we suggest adding 10% to 20% to your final figures. This extra percentage is called a contingency in the field of project management.

When you're done, you'll have all the financial data to prepare a projected income statement. If you use accounting software with features for financial projections, you should create a projected income statement easily. Alternatively, feed your estimated financial data into a spreadsheet-based income statement you can find online.

Step 3: Forecast Your Balance Sheet

The balance sheet is a great tool to figure out how the value of your company changes over time. This will be good to know not only to sell your business but also to manage its debt.

It's easier to use accounting software to prepare your balance sheet forecast because the links between the various financial statements are already in place. Some well-designed accounting spreadsheets can also do the same. However, you need to know what you want to get the right spreadsheets.

Doing a forecast involves identifying assets, liabilities, and shareholders' equity as shown earlier on how to prepare a balance sheet.

Step 4: Prepare a Cash Flow Projection

The last financial projection to forecast is the cash flow by creating an estimated cash flow statement. This projection will be easier to do because you'll source data from the income statement and the balance sheet.

If using accounting software or the right accounting software, the cash flow statement will automatically populate after you've completed the previous two financial statements.

Make sure that your projections cover each month in the first year, quarterly in the second year, and annually thereafter.

Tracking Progress Against Your Projections

While having financial projections is necessary, it doesn't help much if you don't track how your business performs against them. It's like having a family monthly budget that you never use. How is it going to help you stay on track and improve its accuracy going forward? It can't. You need to track your finances.

Your projections tell you what your various business financial goals are. When you monitor your business progress monthly, you'll identify areas where you're falling short. Most importantly, you'll adjust your activities to course-correct. Every quarter, you can make adjustments to your projections. Over time, those financial projections will become more accurate.

One of the aspects of your business finances to pay extra attention to is cash flow. We can't emphasize enough that many small businesses fail because the owners struggle to manage cash. For direct-to-consumer businesses like PoD companies, you sell products for cash. In the early stages of your business, it's very likely that your PoD supplier will want you to pay cash for products. Essentially, your business will be dealing with cash, not credit, meaning that you're going to use cash accounting. This means that you record a transaction when money has either entered or left your bank account.

Your business will struggle with cash management if you make inaccurate business decisions. For instance, if you decide to get into debt to purchase items that the business might not necessarily need, such as a vehicle. Yes, you may deem it necessary to buy a company vehicle, but make sure that this asset brings value to the business—it should generate money for your business. Otherwise, it'll simply be a liability that destroys your cash flow.

As you've noted, we covered a lot of ground in this chapter because it was necessary. It's hard work to create a thriving PoD business, and you can't afford to throw away your success due to poor financial management. Just as marketing and sales are important, so are your finances, especially cash flow. That's why you should have financial projections and track your progress monthly. Only when you have things under control can you start thinking about what we cover in the next chapter, but first, complete the following checklist.

Checklist

	Research and choose an accounting software program. Consider choosing software that offers a free trial to avoid purchasing the wrong one for your needs. Preferably, select accounting software that allows you to create financial projections.
	Create financial projections, beginning with estimating sales and forecast expenses. Out of these figures, your accounting software should churn out the projected income statement, balance sheet, and cash flow statement.
	Track your actual finances against your financial projections. If need be, adjust your projections to mirror your business's financial reality.

Chapter 7:

Business Scaling

Suppose that you've discovered a niche that turns out to be profitable. You now want to scale your business so that you can generate more revenue. This implies that you need to apply business-growing strategies such as selling more of your current products and diversifying your current product offers. The problem is that you're already doing a lot of work in your business. You sleep late to make sure every business activity goes according to plan. Adding more products and customers will burn you out and may even lead to failure.

How do you scale your business and still have enough time to do other things you like? Perhaps you enjoy skiing in Canada during the winters, playing golf, or traveling the world. All these activities need time to do them. The good news is that you can do all these things and more if you know how. This is what this chapter is going to show you.

It Begins With Systemizing Your Processes

A business is a great tool you can use to achieve financial freedom. The business owner is the only one who knows how much their company should make for them to realize that kind of freedom. Many of these business owners need to grow their businesses to a level they can earn this elusive financial freedom. With business growth comes more responsibilities and a lack of time to complete all the work that needs to be done.

Many think that by hiring employees their problems will be solved. Sometimes, this happens, but there's a better approach before thinking about hiring. You need to have business systems so that you can operate your business as efficiently as possible. To understand the value of having business systems, imagine that you took a week's vacation beginning this coming Friday. Will your business keep bringing in the dollars you want, deliver the usual great customer service, and maintain the number of sales leads it attracts? Unless you're one of the rare small business owners, your answer to that question is no.

This section will show you how to turn that answer into an emphatic yes. Perhaps you could even extend your vacation by another week or two. Before we do that, let us share with you the benefits of systemizing your PoD business.

1. **Systems increase business productivity.** Systemizing a business automates routine tasks that maintain its status quo. If these tasks do grow a business, their impact is minimal. When you systemize tasks like these, you have free time to take on needle-moving activities such as introducing a new product line. Perhaps you can use the extra time you now have to improve the quality of the products you offer. These tasks will move your business to a higher revenue level while potentially keeping current customers for longer.

2. **Systems minimize dependence on superstar employees.** If you've hired a couple of employees, there's a chance your business will begin relying on a few of them. Even if you have hired one employee to assist you, your business might depend too much on either you or them. Every person has limitations and may get sick or have other problems that prevent them from working. When you have systems, you'll know exactly what to do to avoid issues. For instance, you may know how to quickly outsource and maintain the required level of production.

3. **Business systems will allow you to work on the business, not only in it.** In the beginning, you work mostly in your business, meaning that you're predominantly the employee. Because of this, you have little time remaining to work on the strategic side of your business. Introducing systems allows you to shift toward doing more of the strategic work, which helps a

great deal when growing your business. Most importantly, you'll free yourself from your business, at which time your company becomes an investment.

4. **Systems enable you to deliver consistent revenue.** It's true that some businesses have seasons. They have months when they generate high revenues, and others when they struggle to break even. Some business owners are quick to blame the seasons without analyzing and finding the real causes. On the other hand, if you have effective marketing and sales systems, you'll generate predictable revenue from one month to the next.

5. **They enhance efficiency.** Systems can eliminate the use of manual labor as often as possible. This not only saves time but also increases efficiency because fewer errors are made. Furthermore, you can easily spot inefficiencies and address them to improve your business processes. As a result, your business will hum much more smoothly and deliver according to expectations.

6. **Systems simplify employee training.** A growing business reaches a point when you can't run it efficiently alone. You simply will have to hire additional employees. Imagine how simpler it will be to induct those employees into your business if you have systems. It'll be a matter of providing the newly hired employee with a detailed job description plus the tools they need to succeed. Within a short time, these employees will start producing at least at the same level you did prior to hiring them.

You'd agree that it's worth creating systems if you want to scale your business higher. As you read the above benefits, you probably began asking yourself, "How do I systematize the processes in my business?" The next section answers that question.

Steps to Systemize Your Business

You can systemize many of the repetitive tasks you do. Where possible, you can use technology to automate them. If you can't use technology, you can outsource and still create free time for yourself. To figure out how to systemize, follow these steps:

Step 1: Identify the Tasks You Do in Your Business

The first step is to figure out all the tasks that you perform in your PoD business. It's easier to do this if you ask yourself questions like these:

- **What does my business do to acquire sales leads?** This question challenges you to look at the specific processes you follow to acquire leads. Yes, perhaps you don't generate leads but prefer to sell directly to your customers. That's okay, but remember that you may be leaving money on the table. Some of your customers might not be ready to buy when you present your offer. Check back in Chapter 4 to remind yourself about how you could generate sales leads.

- **How does my company convert its leads into customers or acquire customers?** You need to know what you do to acquire customers. If you first generate sales leads, you probably run an email sequence to convert some of them into customers. Alternatively, you may be advertising your products directly to your target audience and making sales. Whatever process you follow, note it down. Detail all the sources of your customers, whether social media, search engines, blogs, or ecommerce platforms like Etsy, Amazon, eBay, or Shopify.

- **How does my business fulfill customer orders?** This question requires you to spell out how you get products to your customer timely and efficiently. Even if a third party carries out the fulfillment process, identify what they do from the time they receive an order until the customer receives their product.

- **What does my company do to deliver unparalleled customer service?** This question requires that you identify the steps you take to ensure you deliver excellent customer service. This should include how you handle customer complaints, perform customer service surveys, and ask for reviews.

- **What does my company do to retain customers?** Does your business issue a monthly newsletter? Do you have a loyalty program? Note down all that you do to excite your customer into buying from you more often.

- **How does my business stay on top of its bookkeeping tasks?** What steps do you take to ensure that you complete all your bookkeeping tasks? How often do you do those tasks?

- **What does my business do to manage its cash flows?** How do you ensure that you stay on top of your business' cash flow? Do you review your cash flow weekly, monthly, or quarterly? What do you look for when reviewing your cash flow?

Answering the above questions will be eye-opening. You'll also realize, perhaps for the first time, how much work you do in your business monthly. But identifying the tasks you do in your business is just the beginning.

Step 2: Categorize the Tasks You've Identified

Each of the tasks you've identified in Step 1 can be allocated to a particular category. For example, bookkeeping and review of cash flow belong to the accounting and finance category. Other categories include:

- marketing and sales

- production

- order fulfillment

- customer service

Step 3: Identify the Smaller Steps You Do Per Task

Some of the tasks you've identified in Step 1 may be small enough to keep them as they are. However, some tasks may be bigger. For example, if you use content marketing to generate sales leads, you'll need to break it down further into smaller steps.

Let us illustrate further with the content marketing example. Here may be the smaller steps you take to get leads:

1. Research keywords using Google Trends and Semrush.

2. Select 1 keyword with 1,000 to 5,000 searches per month.

3. Research competitor content to find the number of words they produce in articles targeting the chosen keyword.

4. Brainstorm ways to create content that's better than that of your competitors.

5. Create an outline of the article.

6. Write and edit the article.

7. Publish the article.

As you can see, some steps may require providing additional details depending on its level of complexity. The bottom line is that the major task you identified can be broken down into smaller steps.

Step 4: Identify Tasks That Can Be Systemized

The work you've done in Steps 1 through 3 helped you figure out what tasks you can systemize. These are usually tasks that can be done without too much human intervention. Such tasks can be automated to a large degree.

Relook at the breakdown of each of your major tasks completed in Step 3. Which of those tasks are routine or repetitive? Look closely, and you'll notice that you can systemize tasks such as:

- **Bookkeeping:** This should be easy to systemize by linking your accounting software with your payment processor and bank account. There won't be any need to manually enter financial data into your accounting software.

- **Lead generation:** There's a clear path that a small business can use to acquire sales leads. Because of this, lead generation can be systemized and even automated with technology.

- **Lead conversion to customers:** This task can be systemized and automated the same way as lead generation.

- **Content marketing:** As shown earlier, you can systemize content marketing. If you use social media, you can automate the posting of content to your business pages.

- **Customer service:** You can systemize the nurturing of customers once they've bought a product. This can include persuading them to buy more of your products.

Your list of steps and categories you created will be helpful to identify all the tasks you can systemize.

Step 5: Create SOPs, Checklists, and Templates

Every process has steps to accomplish it. When you have identified the steps involved in each task, which is often a process, you can create SOPs, checklists, and templates. These tools will help you deliver consistent results all the time.

SOPs, templates, and checklists will be helpful when you train new employees. If you can, also include short video demonstrations of how to accomplish certain tasks. Videos will help avoid ambiguity.

For each task, also make sure you spell how long it should take to complete it. In some cases, state how frequently the task should be done.

Nothing deflates like putting a system in place that doesn't deliver the desired results. Imagine having a lead generation system that doesn't bring in the leads! Yes, it may be a system, but it'll be useless as far as revenue generation is concerned.

You can prevent this kind of situation by monitoring how effective each system is. All you do is check if each system gives the results and quality expected.

How to Grow Your Business by Expanding Your Product Line

You've been running your business for months, and you have developed some of the systems you need. While systems are important, they generally don't grow a business but maintain it. Growing or scaling a business involves activities such as expanding your product line or scaling your marketing efforts. In this section, we'll focus on how to scale your business by introducing new products.

Adding a new product to your product line should be seen as introducing a new profit center. This means that you should see the addition of a new product as a business by itself. As such, you'll need to do some of the activities you performed when launching your business for the first time. The main difference is that you're focusing on a product, not a brand. You won't have to find a niche and your brand's value proposition.

Why Expanding Your Product Line Is the Way to Go

Walk into any brick-and-mortar grocery store and what do you notice? You can observe the same thing in an electronics store such as Best Buy or a giant ecommerce store like Amazon.com. The one thing that's common to all these stores is that they offer multiple products. Yet, they didn't start with such large product ranges. This means there must be benefits to introducing additional products in your business. Here are some of the top advantages of doing this:

1. **It improves the overall CX.** Expanding your product line the right way introduces items that your current and future customers want. For instance, if you sell mugs, you may add custom design thermos bottles. This would deliver a great CX to someone looking for a mug and thermos bottle. Users will enjoy shopping in your online store and potentially recommend it to others.

2. **Increases the number and variety of your customers.** When you introduce additional products, you'll likely attract new visitors to your online store. Some of these people will become new customers. As a result, your business will have more and varied types of customers. This opens more opportunities to add new products to your store. For an online business, the number of products you sell is limited by the complexity of your online store. Look at how giant ecommerce businesses such as Alibaba and Amazon have grown. Yours could also reach those proportions if you strategically expand your product line.

3. **It helps successfully ride the challenges of seasonality.** New customers bring in additional revenue you wouldn't have gotten otherwise. The reason is that some products sell only during certain seasons of the year. If you add products that sell throughout the year or in seasons, your current items don't sell well, you'll make the whole year. That's why strategically adding products can be a great decision to make.

4. **It enhances net profit margins.** Expanding your product line can lead to increased net profit margins. As stated above, this would lead to more revenue, and if you keep costs proportionately the same, you'll have more net profits in dollar

terms. These profits could even be higher if you add difficult-to-find products because you can sell them at higher prices.

5. **Expanding product lines leads to increased customer loyalty.** Exceptional customer service and the use of customer loyalty programs can increase customer loyalty. Adding new products to your online store can have the same effect. Think again of a brick-and-mortar grocery store. Would you be thrilled to buy bread in one store and shift to another to buy tea or coffee? Practically, this is possible, but the amount of walking may be tiring. If you can find all the items you need in one store, you won't mind coming back again. Similarly, if you can find all the items in one online store, you'll likely buy them if priced reasonably. As such, increasing your product line can increase customer loyalty.

6. **It increases the average order value.** If you sell one kind of product for $20 apiece and each customer buys one item, the average order value (AOV) is $20. Let's say you add a 2nd product that costs $15 and 10 customers buy it together with the first one. The total each customer spends now becomes $35 for a total store revenue of $350. This means that the AOV jumps to $35, an increase of 50% in this case. Note that this increase will differ based on the prices of your products. Increasing AOV may sound difficult, but it is not because you can sell products that go together like shoes and a pair of socks.

With the benefits of expanding your product line discussed above, can you not do it? It's your choice, but from the scaling of your business angle—it makes sense to do so. It's a question of how to make it happen, which is what we cover next.

Steps for Expanding Your Product Line

Just as you figure out what first product to produce and sell, you should determine what additional products to add. As much as you want to scale your business, it's as important to expand your product line because it's the right thing to do for your customers. If you add products simply because of selfish reasons, you'll likely fail, which is what we DON'T want for you. That's why it's vital to follow the steps mentioned and described below.

Step 1: Set Product Expansion Goals

The results you achieve in business are not accidents, they're the fruits of your labor. To labor that hard, you'll need to know why you do it and what you want to achieve. The same thinking applies when you decide to expand your product line.

Think about why you want to add new products to your online business. Yes, perhaps you want to increase the income you draw from your business, which is fine. However, why do you want your business to grow and what level of growth do you want? This is where product-expansion goals become a necessity. Answer this question, *"Why do I want to expand my business' product line?"*

Your reasons may vary from increasing revenue to increasing the net worth of your business. Whatever your goal is, make sure that you follow the SMART approach as discussed earlier. That's your starting point before moving to the next step.

Step 2: Target Your Audience

When you figured out your ideal buyer, you culminated with creating a buyer persona. It's the work you did that has placed your business in the position it's in today. You also found a product to sell by ensuring that it was what your buyer persona wanted. It follows logically that you should figure out your buyer persona for the new product you want to add.

Instead of the trial-and-error process you followed, you can define your ideal buyer much more accurately for your next product. The reason is that you don't begin by going out to look for customers; you search internally among your current customers for your new buyer persona. This suggests that your starting point is to find out what other products your current customers want. The easiest method to use to find this out is by sending out a survey to your current customers.

First, figure out a list of new products associated with the ones you're currently selling. Brainstorm a couple of product ideas and check if there's market interest in it. This is similar to what you did when you were defining your niche and the product to start your business with. If this sounds hard, you can contact one or two of your customers and ask them what other products they would want that are associated with the ones you currently offer. The list you come up with will be the ones you base your first survey on. After all, your current customers are similar and they probably want similar products.

When creating your survey, ask your customers which of the three or so products they want to be added to your online store. Also, add one or two open-ended questions that tap into the emotions of your customers. For the survey to work, you need to offer the customers you target an incentive to participate. This will help increase the number of participants and make the survey results much more reliable.

Step 3: Conduct a Competitor Product Analysis

Once you have figured out the additional product to include in your business, it's time to study your major competitors. The results of your study and knowledge of your target audience will help you position your product advantageously. Here's how to go about conducting a competitor product analysis.

1. Determine Your Main Objective

Product analysis is broad, and it's easy to go all over when you do it. You can be more targeted if you know what you're specifically evaluating on your competitor products. Since you already know what matters most to your customers, you can choose to focus on the product elements you know interest them the most. Additionally, the market research you did will provide further direction on what to focus on. Whatever objectives you choose to evaluate, don't forget to include quality, price, and customer service.

2. Find Your Competitors

The second step is to identify your competitors. Typically, your competitors fall into three groups: direct competitors, indirect competitors, and replacement competitors.

Direct competitors offer products in the same category or niche as your brand. Their target customers are similar to your buyer persona. You can find numerous PoD competitors on Amazon.com, Etsy, and any other PoD marketplace. Write down a list of the companies that seem to sell the kind of products you offer.

There are also indirect competing brands that sell different products to your type of target audience but in the same category. They could be PoD businesses that sell merchandise that complements what you offer. For instance, these businesses may sell jackets while you offer T-shirts. Companies like these are important to understand because they can easily become your direct competitor.

The third type of competing brands is called replacement competitors. Instead of offering products in your category, they sell ones similar to yours and to your type of market. For instance, they may sell jewelry while you offer hoodies.

The key here is that all these businesses sell to your target audience. Understanding what they sell and why your type of audience buys them could open a profitable opportunity for you.

Since the list of your competitors is probably large, it's worth narrowing it down to a number you can manage. Make sure that you remain with at least five brands after trimming down the list. Most importantly, include brands from all the three competitor groups discussed above.

3. Select Flagship Product From Identified Competitors

Some of your competitors may already be selling multiple products, which can make it difficult for your analysis. To simplify life for yourself, it's a better move to choose one main product from each of your final list of competitors. Typically, this product will be the first that each competitor launches and potentially be bringing in the most sales.

There are numerous product features to explore. We suggest you include the following: style, price, quality, durability, print design, value, and customer service. It's easier if you could create a table like the one below for easy analysis:

Feature	Competitor A	Competitor B	Competitor C
Style			
Price			
Quality			
Durability			
Print design			
Value			
Customer service			

Qualitative features can be tricky to analyze objectively. For this reason, rate each such quality on a scale from 1 to 10, with 10 being the highest quality.

4. Analyze Product Benefits and Shortcomings

This is arguably the most important step in the whole process. It's time to find out why your type of customer buys the products you've chosen to evaluate.

There are two sources of information about your competitor products: the brands themselves and their customers. Study the products pages to learn about the benefits of the products. The important benefits will often be listed first, with the others described later. Some businesses issue product reviews that mention both the advantages and disadvantages of their products. If you can access such reviews, definitely go over them. Other tools that can provide insight into the products include blog posts, videos about the products, and datasheets.

Your competitors will generally lean on the good that their products offer. For a balanced perspective, it's important to find out what others say about the same products. This is where customer reviews and testimonials come in handy. Find out what works and doesn't work for the products' users and note them down. Perhaps you can add a column on the right side of the above table called "customer reviews." Make a note of what customers say about the products against each of the features.

5. Investigate How Your Competitors Market Those Products

One of the most powerful ways of figuring out how your competitors market their products is by analyzing their email campaigns. Many companies offer newsletters or lead magnets on their blogs or social media channels. You can provide your email address in exchange for these kinds of offers, and you'll be added to the company's email list. This is a strategy that has worked for hundreds of years in the direct mail industry. Some marketers think doing this is unethical, which makes you wonder why they even study the competition.

At any rate, getting into your competitor's email campaign gives you a chance to understand how they market their products. Observe what features your competitors focus on emphasizing in their promotions. Are they attracting customers by using discounts, the addition of premiums, or offering unusual guarantees? Check what kind of email sequence they use to convert you into a customer, as well as the frequency of the emails.

Another strategy you can use is studying your competitor's paid ads on social media. Yes, you might not be your competitor's target buyer, but you may access their ads. A platform like Facebook has made it easy for you to access your competitor's ads. This came about because Facebook wanted to increase transparency. All you do is visit your competitor's Facebook page, select "Page Transparency," then "See All," and finally click the "Go to Ad Library" button. You'll be taken to your competitor's Facebook Ad Library, a great resource for finding out what ads work and what features your competitors promote.

Tools like Semrush and SimilarWeb also provide a way to study your competitor's ads. The good news is that you can use these platforms for free for a limited time on a trial basis. Don't forget about search engines like Bing and Google. By simply entering the right keywords, you may find your competitor ads and study them.

At this point, you should have a good handle on what kind of product to create and what minimum features it should have. Most importantly, you should be clear on how to position your product advantageously.

Step 4: Create a Prototype

All the work you've completed thus far has prepared you for this step. It's time to build a product prototype that has the features your target buyer desires. A prototype is a sample product you want to introduce to the market. The power of a prototype is that it prevents you from investing tons of money into an idea that's not proven in the market.

There's a reason big and popular companies such as Apple, Microsoft, and Toyota don't aim to produce the final product from the start. Consider the iPhone. It was first launched in 2007, but Apple had been working on it for about 3 years before launching it. When you think about it, there's no product that meets every customer's wants and needs.

That's why there can be many versions of a product as the manufacturer discovers more and more what its customers want. The first iPhone went through numerous iterations before it was ready for the market. Even software companies produce what they called a beta product before finalizing their software. This iteration refines the product until it's good enough.

It's easy to create a prototype PoD product. Simply select the kind of product you want to sell and create the design. Stick the design onto the product. Then add the product to your online store. However, before listing the product in your store, first, get a couple of its samples for evaluation. Send some of them to your customers for free in exchange for a review. Make it clear to them that you want their thoughts about the product for improvement purposes. Of course, also get one of the samples.

Use the feedback to make improvements. For example, you may need to change the type of printing, the image, the design, or the kind of material. Once you've made the changes, get samples again and send them to the same customers. Repeat this process until about 60% to 80% of the customers are happy with the product. At that point, you're ready for the next step.

Step 5: Test-Launch Your Prototype

You now have a prototype that some of your customers like. However, this doesn't necessarily mean you've successfully added a new product to your store. After all, the people who tested your product got it for free.

The big test is getting someone to whip out their wallet and buy your prototype. You can find out quickly if you have customers who like and buy your prototype. All it takes is simply making them an offer and seeing what happens.

What you do is add your final prototype to your online store. Then create an offer and send it to your existing list of customers. The key here isn't about making a profit, but proving that the market for your new product exists. In line with this, offer the product at cost to avoid losing money on it. This means that if your product and shipping cost $30, you offer the product for $30 apiece.

If some of your customers buy your prototype, you know you're in business. Most importantly, you know who your ideal customer is. If you're unsure who your buyers are, you can check their profiles because you already have them. Once done, you may proceed to the next step.

Step 6: Plan the Launch of Your Product

Congratulations on successfully finding a new product to add to your online store. The next activity to do is officially launch the new product. This requires having a marketing strategy for the product. Here's how to proceed with the preparation:

1. **Define your launch goal.** How many items would you need to sell to consider your launch successful? Perhaps you're not concerned with making sales right away but are interested in creating sales opportunities or building awareness. Whatever it is you want to achieve should be clear and be SMART, as discussed earlier. The goals you set will dictate what you do and to what extent. Don't forget to set the date for your product launch.

2. **Create promotional material.** It's now time to create promotional material that will enable you to reach your goals. The kind of material you develop will depend on the marketing channels you're going to use. If you want to use YouTube, you could create video material targeted to attract your kind of customer. For social media, you'll create the kind of content suited to the platform and your target customer. You may prefer to use email marketing together with social media platforms. That's fine, but remember to create a method for generating leads and an email series to nurture those leads and convert them into customers.

Depending on how you want to sell your product, it may be necessary to publish your promotional material a few weeks before the launch. For instance, you may publish content on social media and promote it to get your target market ready to buy when you launch your product. Launching your product is straightforward if you use paid ads. All it takes is to prepare your ads and make sure your online store works. You can't afford to make mistakes when you launch your product.

After you've launched your product, you'll have sales numbers and expenses to create the product and fulfill orders. You also have data that'll enable you to analyze the performance of your promotional material. Evaluate this data and determine how well your launch worked. Remember to compare the results you achieved with the goals you set above.

If your launch succeeds, you would have added a new product to your online store. What's left is to accelerate its sales, meaning that you need to keep promoting your new product just as you did with your initial one.

How to Find Areas for Potential Revenue Increase and Growth

What if you don't want to introduce a new product line to scale your business? Can you still increase revenue and profits from the same products you currently have? You bet. What it takes is knowing what to do. This section's purpose is to show you how to scale without adding a new product. Before we introduce you to what you should do, let us make a few crucial points.

Scaling any business involves doing one of three things:

- increasing the number of customers

- getting your customers to buy more often

- increasing the average order size of your customer purchases

Adding new products to your online store can lead to increased order size and number of customers. Whether your customers buy more will depend on the kind of merchandise you sell. Items like food, cosmetics, and supplements are great for getting your customers to buy regularly. This is because customers have to replenish them regularly. In the PoD industry, you'll rely mostly on selling different kinds of items to get customers to buy more often, which you'll achieve by adding new products to your store.

Let's now turn our attention to strategies you can implement to scale your business without adding new products.

Collaborate With Other Businesses

Do you want to acquire new leads and customers without spending a dime? If so, consider collaborating with other brands. This is a great way to increase the visibility of your business. If done well, it might turn out to be the simplest way to acquire customers.

Imagine that your online store offers clothing, and you want to take your sales to the next level. You're aware that your local football club, the Giant Killers, is popular in the community. After carefully thinking about how to benefit from that popularity, you approach the team and ask for a collaboration. The Giant Killers like how they'll benefit from the partnership. You both agree to introduce a new sneaker featuring the Giant Killers's logo and your design.

You launch the sneaker, and followers of the Giant Killers buy them like there's no tomorrow. Both the Giant Killers and your brand are happy. Yet, this is just the beginning. There are more opportunities to promote the sneaker to other customers that don't follow the Giant Killers.

What you've just read is one way of collaborating with other brands to grow your business. The great thing is that you can do it for free. To understand the mechanics of collaborations, let's dive deeper into how they work.

Why You Should Do Brand Collaborations

Participating in a partnership with another brand provides benefits that could be hard to get in any other way. Some of the top ways these collaborations are advantageous include the following:

1. **Increasing brand awareness.** You can access the other company's customers. When your collaborator touts your business and products, their customers are likely to pay attention. The reason is that there's already a relationship that exists between your partner and their customers.

2. **Making more sales and cheaper.** Increased brand awareness can lead to increased sales. Most importantly, such sales can come at a cheaper price. The reason is that brand collaboration is 1/25 times the cost of digital advertising. As a result, if you acquire a customer for $20 from a digital channel, it'll cost you $0.80 to achieve the same thing with brand collaboration. This alone makes it worthwhile to consider brand collaboration.

3. **Avails resources that are too expensive for your brand.** Let's say that your brand has to pay a designer to design your artwork for the items you sell. As you know, hiring a freelance or full-time designer can come at a huge price. What if you partner with a design company in exchange for certain resources you have? You could save yourself several thousands of dollars, and perhaps the same may be true for your partnering brand.

If enjoying the above benefits interests you, read on to learn more about forging brand collaborations.

A brand collaboration is the partnering of two or more companies to increase sales and engagement for both of them. The partnership can work provided the collaborating business complement each other.

Every business has resources and assets that can be beneficial to other companies. For instance, it has customers that may also be interested in the products another company sells. For instance, a brand that sells kitchen appliances may collaborate with another that offers PoD mugs and plates.

Finding Brand Collaborators

How do you find brands you can collaborate with? In the modern age, finding the brand you want is simpler due to the technology available. But, before you begin the process of looking for brands you can collaborate with, you need to set goals.

1. Set Goals

The starting point of any initiative is to define your goals so that you can do the right activities and measure your success. So, establish the goals you want to achieve by collaborating, making sure they're SMART goals. For instance, your goal may be to increase sales by 20% by the end of the year through brand collaborations.

2. Find the Right Brands

Strange as it may sound, you can be the best in your industry and not get one company to approach you for collaboration. Brand collaboration will not happen by itself, it needs you to reach out for it—you have to be proactive, rather than passive.

There are numerous sources to locate possible brands to collaborate with. The quickest method is to search for them online. Think about brands that complement the products you sell. What are the keywords that customers use to search for the products or services? Enter them in a search engine and go through the results that come up. Don't rule out any of them yet. Simply add each of the brands to your list. Go to social media platforms and search for other brands.

Select 15 to 20 brands out of your list that you can contact and propose a collaboration. It's easier to find decision-makers in smaller companies, which means you should focus on such brands for now. It's now time to research the brands you've chosen.

For each brand, learn what it does, what it stands for, and what it hopes to achieve. Find out what's the main product they sell and, if possible, how well it is selling. If they have a blog, check their articles and pick one or two that interest them. Don't worry, there's a reason for doing this you'll know shortly. Also, find out what accomplishments each brand has had, preferably recently.

Armed with this research, go ahead and plan how to reach them and what you say. In your planning, think about what to say to them. As you do so, remember that you want to add value to the other brand. This is what the other brand wants to hear, not that you want to collaborate and increase your sales. You should think about what to offer them in exchange for the collaboration.

Once you have the plan, find out who to contact. It must be the decision-maker so that both of you can move ahead quicker. You can find the decision-maker on social media platforms such as LinkedIn.

When you have a plan and the name and contact details of the decision-maker, it's time to write to them. Introduce your brand and what you do, and then mention that you liked their certain blog. Go on to say that you believe their company could increase their sales if you allowed them to market their products to your customers. Of course, what you offer will depend on what you think is important to them. Don't go into too much detail because the other party should first respond to your initial perspective.

The possible response you might get is having a meeting. Don't let this scare you because you can hold online meetings instead of physical ones. That's when you can begin collaboration discussions.

3. *Discuss the Scope of the Collaboration*

All you're looking for is to find just one brand to collaborate with. Out of those you contact, a few may respond positively. Those are the ones you move with to the next stage, which is to discuss the scope of the collaboration.

The first thing you should agree on is how the collaboration will benefit either of the brands. When it's clear that the collaboration will be mutually beneficial, it's time to set goals—collaboration objectives.

The next thing to agree upon is the type of collaboration you'll have. There are three types of brand collaborations: co-marketing, product collaboration, and influencer marketing. If you're collaborating with another business, the kind of collaboration you'll probably go for is co-marketing or product collaboration. Influencer marketing works primarily between a business and an individual with a large following, especially on social media.

Co-marketing is when your brand and its partner take advantage of their reputation to benefit each other. It involves each of the brands marketing the other's products to its customers and even sales leads. However, the two brands shouldn't be direct competitors. Product collaboration is what we introduced this topic with. Two brands combine to create a product that has the fingerprints of both.

It's vital to be clear about what each brand is going to do and what resources it will commit to the cause. By definition, a collaboration is a project, meaning that it has a start and an end. As such, you should agree with your collaborator on the timeline.

4. *Sign a Collaboration Agreement*

After agreeing on the type of collaboration, create an agreement that states the terms, conditions, and responsibilities of each party. The agreement should address intellectual rights (if any) and financial contributions, if needed.

The key is making sure each brand is protected in the collaboration. You may need to consult a legal expert to help you with such an agreement.

5. Execute Your Part of the Agreement

Your next task is to execute your responsibilities as set in the collaboration agreement. Typically, that will include creating marketing collateral that the other party can send to their audience. Additionally, you'll need to craft an offer for your collaborator's customer base.

It's a good idea to consider generating leads instead of going straight for sales. Once you have the leads, you can market to them over and over again. Contrast this with trying to get customers right away. If you don't succeed, you're surely going to miss out on possible sales later in the relationship.

Your brand collaborator should do their part.

6. Launch the Collaboration

When both of you are ready, kick off the collaboration. Most importantly, monitor how the collaborative process progresses by measuring the metrics identified when setting goals. If issues arise, resolve them immediately.

7. Assess the Results

Organize your results from the collaborative efforts. Then, analyze how the collaboration performed against the goals set at the start. Was there an improvement in sales, brand awareness, or engagement?

The results from this collaboration will help improve future ones.

Unless you're a copywriter, there's a chance that your marketing material isn't as effective as it can be. Understand that a copywriter is a salesperson who uses the written word to sell products or services. The kind of copywriter you need is one who is versed in marketing. That way, you'll get the best of both worlds: marketing strategy and execution and optimization of your content and sales material.

A good copywriter knows how to write persuasive content and advertisements. For instance, they write product descriptions that influence the reader to buy what you sell. This is particularly important in digital marketing, which is what you use when you run an online store. The reason is that good digital marketing revolves around persuading the reader to take some action, such as clicking on a link.

Here are good reasons for hiring a copywriter with a knack for marketing:

- **They'll boost your conversions.** There are two types of conversions if your strategy involves generating leads before creating customers. The first is converting strangers into leads. A copywriter knows how to influence such people into biting on the bait you use to attract leads. If your offer isn't strong, they'll help you make it more powerful. Additionally, they'll write sales copy that's persuasive to get your target audience to act as you want. Similarly, they work on your email sequence to get it to convert more of your leads to customers. Thus, you'll generate more customers and, potentially, get them to buy more of your products.

- **A good copywriter crafts persuasive copy.** The words you use in your marketing material can hurt your sales. Fortunately, a good copywriter knows the words and phrases needed to influence a person. When you hire them, they spend time studying your target audience, customers, and the competition to craft persuasive copy. You need persuasive social media posts, product pages, blog posts, and any other content. Make sure that you check the results that your copywriter has produced for others to avoid hiring wrongly.

- **You'll have more time to focus on other business activities.** By now, you should have realized that it can be challenging to create marketing content and sales material. If you hire a good copywriter, you'll have more time to perform functions such as adding new products and forging brand collaborations. When you combine the effect of these interventions on your revenues, it'll be worth hiring a copywriter.

Imagine that your marketing material produces $50,000 in annual revenue. Let's further say that your sales copy converted 0.9% to bring that revenue. If you hire a copywriter who can increase your conversion by 50%, the new conversion will be 1.35%. As such, your revenue can jump to $75,000 ($50,000 x 1.35/0.9) per year, all things constant. Isn't that something worth doing?

Create an Abandoned Cart Email Sequence

Imagine that a potential customer visits your online store and adds the product you sell to the shopping cart. For some unknown reason, they don't complete their purchase. Without a doubt, this can be frustrating, especially if you have numerous people doing this. The good news is that you can reduce the rate at which people abandon your shopping cart. Before explaining how to do this, let us explain this.

As you probably know by now, you can't improve any metric unless you first measure it. The same applies to cart abandonment. The metric used to determine this measure is called cart abandonment rate, and you calculate it as follows:

Cart abandonment rate = 100 − cart completion rate

Where cart completion rate is the ratio of the number of completed purchases to the number of shopping carts created, expressed in percentage.

When given in formula form:

$$\text{Cart completion rate} = \text{number of completed purchases}/\text{Number of shopping carts created} \times 100$$

The higher the shopping cart completion rate, the lower the cart abandonment rate. In the US, nearly 57% of carts are abandoned, which is a huge figure. If you could cut that figure by half, you'll make about 24 additional sales per 100 people who created a shopping cart. Even if you don't reach such a high reduction and only achieve a 20% reduction, you'll make 11 more sales.

There are numerous strategies you can use to cut down the number of cart abandonments. The most popular include the following:

- Offering free shipping.

- Giving customers multiple payment options and making sure the popular ones are available.

- Simplify your checkout process. The more complex you make it, the quicker buyers get frustrated and leave your shopping cart.

- Making sure that your checkout is secure.

There's still one more tactic you can apply if all the above fail: Create a cart abandonment email sequence. Your email sequence should have at least two emails. Creating only one email might not be effective, while too many may feel like you're pushing it.

Most importantly, don't settle for good enough results. Keep an open mind for opportunities to scale. Networking with like-minded entrepreneurs and reading good business books will help uncover such opportunities.

To conclude this chapter, complete the following checklist.

Checklist

	Create systems such as standard operating procedures, checklists, and templates for all your business operations, including marketing and sales, order fulfillment, production, and finances.
	Research and select a new product to add to your business. Remember to study your competition, identify your ideal target audience, and create a prototype before launching your new product.
	Research and locate brands (including companies and individuals) you can collaborate with to expand the reach of your business.
	Hire a copywriter adept with marketing to improve your marketing material and enhance lead generation and customer acquisition.
	Create an email series consisting of at least two emails to convert some of the people who don't complete their purchase in your online store. Avoiding too many emails in your sequence.

Conclusion

We all need reminding sometimes, especially about unfamiliar topics. While many have seen customized T-shirts, hoodies, phone cases, and mugs, they have not yet learned the business side of such products. As you've noted, this book guides you on how to create and build a business that sells such products. It's worth reminding yourself about what you learned as you build your PoD business.

Where do you start when building a PoD business? You always begin with learning the fundamentals. In this case, it means understanding that a PoD business creates a product once the customer has paid for it. There's no need to keep an inventory of finished products. Ideally, you outsource production and order fulfillment to a third-party company. The PoD approach is great when you want to test a new product idea, expand your product line, or monetize your social media following or any other following such as an email list.

Another key aspect of starting a PoD business is understanding that you need to have an online store. Common ecommerce platforms for hosting such a store include Amazon and Etsy. You can integrate your store with a PoD platform that may also fulfill your orders, such as Printful and Printify.

With the fundamentals taken care of, your next step is to find a small segment of a broad market called a niche. Selling to this narrow market segment is cheaper and allows you to build a reputation and brand loyalty quickly. To enjoy your business, first, explore your passions and interests and then find a market that aligns with them. You also need to research the competition to find weaknesses you can take advantage of.

From this research, define a buyer persona who your PoD business will sell to, as well as the value you'll provide to them. Additionally, define your brand and its associated elements such as messaging, logo, fonts, and colors.

When you're certain that there's a market, it's time to look for a product to sell. A good product should be in demand and, preferably, be evergreen. Places like Amazon's Best Sellers list and Etsy are some excellent places to discover in-demand products. You can also begin your product search by taking popular items such as hoodies, T-shirts, mugs, and phone accessories and checking if they're selling well on ecommerce marketplaces.

Once you have found the product to sell, you need to get its white-label version manufactured. That's when you begin the search for a manufacturer or supplier. In your search, make sure that whichever manufacturer you choose can deliver quality products. Some great places to find potential manufacturers include Printful, Redbubble, and Printify. When you find a manufacturer, get samples to verify quality before you sign an agreement with them. It's worth partnering with more than one manufacturer to build redundancy in your supply chain and have a plan B when one of them faces delays.

Some manufacturers may also fulfill your customers' orders. It's worth outsourcing this business function if you're not an expert at it. Doing so allows you to reach a wider audience and ship products quicker. When you seek an order fulfillment company, consider factors such as lead times, ecommerce integration, customer support, location, and product quality.

You now know where to find a white-label product to sell. What happens next? You sell the final product decked with your custom design in your online store. This needs proper marketing and sales. Understanding the customer journey plays an essential role in how you market.

The first three stages of the customer journey (awareness, consideration, and decision) correspond with the four steps of a marketing funnel (attention, interest, desire, and action). You need to identify where your potential customers are in the customer journey and market to them accordingly. Once they buy, you still need to market to them to retain and turn them into loyal customers.

At the center of your marketing lies your marketing strategy and plans. It might be necessary in the beginning to refine your marketing strategy and plans to get the results you need. This is why you need to measure the performance of your marketing strategy and plans. For optimal marketing performance, include email marketing to convert leads into customers.

Of course, when customers buy your product, you'll need to fulfill their orders. If you outsource this function as proposed in Chapter 3, your partner will handle all the necessary tasks. Still, it's essential to understand what goes on behind the scenes of order fulfillment. Have your supplier provide an action plan to handle order fulfillment issues such as production delays, poor-quality products, supply chain problems, and inventory management failures. Consider optimization of order fulfillment.

Marketing and sales also bring money into your bank account. Managing this money is as crucial as every other task for creating a successful PoD business. The main metric to keep track of is cash flow—the difference between incoming and outgoing money. Financial planning involves preparing projections and tracking income and expenses. This is accomplished by using the income statement, cash flow statement, and balance sheet. Using accounting software simplifies financial planning and management.

The time comes when you want to expand your PoD business. Before doing this, you need to systemize your business, which demands that you first stabilize it. Systemizing a business starts with writing down all the steps you perform to produce a particular result. Having a system for each of your business functions ensures that you produce consistent outcomes and stops you from relying on certain employees. For example, a marketing system delivers customers of a certain quality, leading to consistent revenue.

When you have systems, you can move ahead and expand your product line. This is the quickest method of increasing revenue and profit. Your systems will allow you to do this without increasing the time you work in your business too much. Other methods of scaling your venture include collaborating with other brands, optimizing your marketing material by hiring an effective copywriter, and reducing your shopping cart abandonment rate.

While this book provided the steps you need to build a profitable PoD business, it's crucial to follow through. You'll need to push yourself harder because learning and doing new things requires breaking old barriers. Your major investment in your PoD business is your time because you don't need tons of upfront money. As long as you have some money, an internet device like a laptop or mobile phone, and a great business idea, you'll get it right.

Enjoy building your PoD business!

Before you go, we just wanted to say thank you for purchasing our book. You could have picked from dozens of other books on the same topic but you took a chance and chose this one. So, a HUGE thanks to you for getting this book and for reading all the way to the end.

Now, we wanted to ask you for a small favor. COULD YOU PLEASE CONSIDER POSTING A REVIEW ON THE PLATFORM? (Reviews are one of the easiest ways to support the work of independent authors.)

This feedback will help us continue to write the type of books that will help you get the results you want. So if you enjoyed it, please let us know!

We wish you much Success on your Journey!

Made in United States
Orlando, FL
26 February 2024

44121124R00098